WITHDRAWN

THE CENTRAL INTELLIGENCE AGENCY

Other books in the At Issue series:

Alcohol Abuse
Animal Experimentation
Anorexia
The Attack on America: September 11, 2001
Biological and Chemical Weapons
Bulimia
Cloning
Creationism vs. Evolution
Does Capital Punishment Deter Crime?
Drugs and Sports
Drunk Driving
The Ethics of Abortion
The Ethics of Genetic Engineering
The Ethics of Human Cloning
Heroin
Home Schooling
How Can Gun Violence Be Reduced?
How Should Prisons Treat Inmates?
Human Embryo Experimentation
Is Global Warming a Threat?
Islamic Fundamentalism
Is Media Violence a Problem?
Legalizing Drugs
Missile Defense
National Security
Nuclear and Toxic Waste
Nuclear Security
Organ Transplants
Performance-Enhancing Drugs
Physician-Assisted Suicide
Police Corruption
Professional Wrestling
Rain Forests
Satanism
School Shootings
Should Abortion Rights Be Restricted?
Should There Be Limits to Free Speech?
Teen Sex
Video Games
What Encourages Gang Behavior?
What Is a Hate Crime?
White Supremacy Groups

THE CENTRAL INTELLIGENCE AGENCY

Helen Cothran, *Book Editor*

Daniel Leone, *President*
Bonnie Szumski, *Publisher*
Scott Barbour, *Managing Editor*

San Diego • Detroit • New York • San Francisco • Cleveland
New Haven, Conn. • Waterville, Maine • London • Munich

© 2003 by Greenhaven Press. Greenhaven Press is an imprint of The Gale Group, Inc., a division of Thomson Learning, Inc.

Greenhaven® and Thomson Learning™ are trademarks used herein under license.

For more information, contact
Greenhaven Press
27500 Drake Rd.
Farmington Hills, MI 48331-3535
Or you can visit our Internet site at http://www.gale.com

ALL RIGHTS RESERVED.
No part of this work covered by the copyright hereon may be reproduced or used in any form or by any means—graphic, electronic, or mechanical, including photocopying, recording, taping, Web distribution or information storage retrieval systems—without the written permission of the publisher.

Every effort has been made to trace the owners of copyrighted material.

LIBRARY OF CONGRESS CATALOGING-IN-PUBLICATION DATA

The Central Intelligence Agency / Helen Cothran, book editor.
p. cm. — (At issue)
Includes bibliographical references and index.
ISBN 0-7377-1725-4 (hb : alk. paper) — ISBN 0-7377-1726-2 (pbk. : alk. paper)
1. United States. Central Intelligence Agency. 2. Terrorism. 3. Violence.
I. Cothran, Helen. II. At issue (San Diego, Calif.)
JK468.I6 C4545 2003
327.1273—dc21 2002029722

Printed in the United States of America

Contents

Introduction

After Islamic extremists hijacked four commercial airliners and deliberately crashed three of them into the World Trade Center and the Pentagon on September 11, 2001, many commentators noted that America would never be the same. Time will tell if those observers prove correct, but one thing is for sure: The government agencies responsible for national security will never be the same. Indeed, although many analysts argue that America's intelligence agencies could not have prevented such a well-orchestrated attack, many people immediately began to blame the CIA for the tragedy. They wanted an accounting of the CIA's failure to predict and prevent the attack and called for changes in the way the CIA conducts business. As Jack Citrin, a professor of political science at the University of California at Berkeley, puts it, "People are asking, 'Why didn't [U.S. intelligence agencies] prevent this from happening? Were they asleep at the wheel?'" A May 2002 Gallup poll found that only 20 percent of respondents had a very positive view of the CIA. Recent criticisms leveled at the CIA are hardly new, however. In fact, the agency has had a troubled history almost since its inception.

The CIA was created in 1947 by President Harry S. Truman as a component of the National Security Act, which also created the Defense Department and the National Security Council. Truman wanted an agency that would collect, synthesize, and analyze information about other nations, especially America's enemies, so that the United States would never again be caught off guard as it had been when the Japanese bombed Pearl Harbor in December 1941. Intelligence gathering did not begin with the CIA's creation, however. In fact, the United States had conducted espionage as far back as the Revolutionary War, and the first formal intelligence agencies, which were run by the military, were created in the 1880s. In addition, during World War II, President Franklin D. Roosevelt established the Office of Strategic Services (OSS), which was charged with collecting intelligence and engaging in covert action. The OSS, however, was abolished when World War II ended.

As Truman envisioned it, the CIA's job was to coordinate the nation's intelligence activities and correlate, evaluate, and disseminate intelligence that affected national security. In essence, the CIA works for the president, assisting the administration in making foreign policy decisions. Very quickly, the CIA became America's front line in its war against communism. During the Cold War, the CIA was charged with monitoring Soviet weapons capabilities using spy planes, ships, and satellites. The agency also planned covert operations in an attempt to influence the political processes in Communist countries.

Not long into the CIA's war against communism, the agency suffered its first major debacle, the Bay of Pigs. In 1961, the CIA covertly helped Cuban exiles invade Cuba in an attempt to oust Communist leader Fidel

Castro. The invasion was a failure, however, and Castro's forces routed the exiles. The CIA was criticized on the one hand for failing to remove Castro from power and on the other hand for engaging in covert operations, which are always controversial. Simultaneously, the agency was being represented as an ineffectual government bureaucracy and an unaccountable behemoth violating the foundations of an open society.

The first major investigation into CIA wrongdoing occurred during the Cold War in 1975. Senator Frank Church of Idaho led a special investigation that uncovered systematic abuse within the agency, including spying on U.S. citizens and plotting to assassinate foreign leaders such as Castro and Congolese premier Patrice Lumumba. The committee released a damning report, in which Church called the CIA "a rogue elephant rampaging out of control." The Church committee report also prompted President Gerald Ford to sign an executive order that banned U.S. officials from carrying out or aiding in assassinations.

Another investigation into CIA wrongdoing that began during the Cold War was conducted by a reporter named Gary Webb, who eventually published his findings in a series for the *San Jose Mercury News*. Webb's series, called Dark Alliance, was later made into a book by the same name; it alleged that the CIA was involved in drug trafficking. Webb charged that drug traffickers were selling crack cocaine to poor Los Angeles neighborhoods in the 1980s and funneling the profits to the Nicaragua Contras, whom the CIA was helping to overthrow the Communist Sandinista regime. According to Webb, the CIA was aware of those transactions, and did nothing to stop them. Webb's accusations prompted the CIA to conduct an internal investigation, the report of which was finally published in 1998. The CIA considered the report an absolution of any wrongdoing in the Contra-cocaine affair, despite Webb's insistence to the contrary.

Major CIA fiascoes did not end with the Cold War. In fact, the collapse of the Soviet Union in 1991 began an era of systematic U.S. intelligence failures. The first criticism leveled at the CIA during this post–Cold War era was that the CIA had failed to predict the demise of the Soviet Union. Critics voiced concern that if the agency lacked crucial intelligence concerning the viability of the one nation on which it had spent most of its resources monitoring, things did not bode well for the agency's ability to respond to new threats developing after the Cold War. Indeed, subsequent intelligence failures revealed a CIA mired in Cold War intelligence methods and ill-equipped to handle new threats. For one thing, the CIA still considered communism—not terrorism—the most serious threat to U.S. security, and began focusing on China rather than the Middle East. Moreover, the methods that the CIA was using had been developed to deal with one major state enemy and its sphere of influence. The CIA had become reliant on sophisticated technology such as listening devices that worked effectively when enemies held counsel with one another in conference rooms. However, the CIA's technology proved virtually useless in monitoring the activities of roving bands of terrorists. In addition, while it had been relatively easy to bribe disgruntled Soviet workers to spy on their government on behalf of the United States, the CIA found that terrorist cells were tightly knit and hard to infiltrate.

Perhaps the most important weakness was that CIA agents themselves seemed ill-suited to operate in the new era. For example, many CIA operatives could speak fluent Russian, but what was now needed were agents who could speak Middle Eastern languages, such as Arabic. Many agents also found the prospect of infiltrating terrorist cells—which often requires living among the terrorists in filth, poverty, and danger—highly undesirable. Indeed, many critics accuse CIA agents of getting soft. Many contend that CIA employees began to care more about their paychecks and retirement benefits than serving their country.

In part because of the CIA's resistance to change, the agency experienced additional intelligence gaffes in the post–Cold War era. For example, it took nine years to arrest CIA agent Aldrich Ames for spying for the Soviet Union. In a comment about the affair, the Senate Select Committee on Intelligence characterized the CIA as "a bureaucracy excessively tolerant of serious personal and professional misconduct among its employees." In addition, it was revealed in 1995 that Guatemalan military officials associated with the CIA were involved in murdering U.S. citizens. This revelation prompted the CIA to establish guidelines on the use of sources having a history of human rights abuses. Also, in May 1998, the CIA failed to detect India's nuclear weapons testing, an oversight that Alabama senator Richard Shelby called "a colossal failure of our intelligence agencies." India's success in developing and testing nuclear weapons led to a mini arms race between India and Pakistan that threatens nuclear security worldwide. In addition, many critics blame the CIA for the bombing of what the agency thought was a chemical weapons factory in Khartoum, Sudan, in 1998. In May 1999, the CIA was implicated in the errant bombing of the Chinese embassy in Belgrade, Yugoslavia, during the campaign to force Serbs out of Kosovo. CIA director George Tenet said of the bombing, "It was a major error." What has become for many the most egregious intelligence failure of all time, however, is the September 11 terrorist attacks.

In the aftermath of the attacks, the CIA has undergone significant change. With the passage of the USA-PATRIOT Act in October 2001, the CIA has been granted expanded powers, including increased latitude in information gathering on U.S. citizens. The CIA is now permitted to monitor the Internet activity and telephone conversations of suspected terrorists, for example. In addition, information gleaned from grand jury proceedings and criminal investigations is now to be shared with the CIA.

Many civil rights groups fear that these new powers will add to increased wrongdoing and reduced accountability. Stanford history professor Barton Bernstein says, "Over the years, [CIA personnel] have been malevolent, and in the short run they have often been inept. So to give them more power and more resources and less accountability seems rather dangerous." In contrast, supporters believe that the changes are necessary to facilitate communication between the FBI, the CIA, and other agencies. Many believe that a lack of cooperation and communication between America's various law enforcement and intelligence agencies is largely responsible for the September 11 attacks. As *San Francisco Chronicle* reporter Louis Freedberg explains, "Defenders of [intelligence] agencies say it is unfair to lump the missteps together to paint a broad picture of incompetence. Each mistake has separate roots, often in different branches and departments of various intelligence agencies."

Many analysts feel that the changes already made within the intelligence community do not go far enough. They call for a complete restructuring of America's intelligence agencies. The cabinet-level Department of Homeland Security proposed by President George W. Bush in June 2002 may play a significant role in such a reorganization. Other observers argue that the CIA should be expanded, which would necessitate the allocation of more federal money to the agency. Along the same lines, some analysts contend that the ban on assassinations and the regulations regarding the recruitment of sources with histories of human rights abuses should be rescinded. Many are also talking about allowing the CIA to use torture. These observers believe that restrictions on assassinations, recruitment, and torture hamper the CIA's ability to infiltrate and abolish terrorist cells.

The sense of security that had developed during an era of relative peace and prosperity came abruptly to an end as the twin towers collapsed in September 2001. It is certainly no surprise that Americans began to wonder why the CIA had not protected them from the Islamic terrorists bent on their destruction. In *At Issue: The CIA*, professors, government officials, civil rights activists, and journalists debate whether or not the CIA was responsible for the terrorist attacks on America and how the agency should change in response to these new threats to America's security. Realistic or not, Americans expect the CIA to protect them from such tragedies on their soil. Time will tell whether the CIA will succeed in meeting these expectations or whether its troubled history will continue.

1

The CIA Is Responsible for the Terrorist Attacks on America

Massimo Calabresi and Romesh Ratnesar

Massimo Calabresi is an intelligence correspondent for Time. *Romesh Ratnesar is a staff writer for the same magazine.*

There are many reasons why the CIA failed to anticipate and prevent the September 11, 2001, terrorist attacks on America. First, the CIA still functions as it did during the Cold War, but the threats to America's national security have changed radically since the Soviet Union collapsed. While the CIA still has numerous agents who speak fluent Russian, for instance, the war on terrorism requires operatives who speak Middle Eastern languages. Second, the U.S. intelligence community spends the majority of its budget on technology, such as satellites and eavesdropping gadgets, but this technology is not suited to track terrorists such as those responsible for the September 11 attacks. Third, America's intelligence community is divided into several agencies that do not communicate effectively with one another, which often allows terrorists to slip through the cracks. Collaboration between U.S. intelligence agencies and substantive changes in CIA tactics will be essential in fighting America's new enemies.

For a few harrowing weeks last fall [2001], a group of U.S. officials believed that the worst nightmare of their lives—something even more horrific than [the September 11 terrorist attacks on America]—was about to come true. In October an intelligence alert went out to a small number of government agencies, including the Energy Department's top-secret Nuclear Emergency Search Team, based in Nevada. The report said that terrorists were thought to have obtained a 10-kiloton nuclear weapon from the Russian arsenal and planned to smuggle it into New York City. The source of the report was a mercurial agent code-named DRAGONFIRE, who intelligence officials believed was of "undetermined" reliabil-

From "Can We Stop the Next Attack?" by Massimo Calabresi and Romesh Ratnesar, *Time*, March 11, 2002. Copyright © 2002 by Time, Inc. Reprinted with permission.

ity. But DRAGONFIRE's claim tracked with a report from a Russian general who believed his forces were missing a 10-kiloton device. Since the mid-'90s, proliferation experts have suspected that several portable nuclear devices might be missing from the Russian stockpile. That made the DRAGONFIRE report alarming. So did this: detonated in lower Manhattan, a 10-kiloton bomb would kill some 100,000 civilians and irradiate 700,000 more, flattening everything in a half-mile diameter. And so counterterrorist investigators went on their highest state of alert.

"It was brutal," a U.S. official told *Time*. It was also highly classified and closely guarded. Under the aegis of the White House's Counterterrorism Security Group, part of the National Security Council, the suspected nuke was kept secret so as not to panic the people of New York. Senior FBI officials were not in the loop. Former mayor Rudolph Giuliani says he was never told about the threat. In the end, the investigators found nothing and concluded that DRAGONFIRE's information was false. But few of them slept better. They had made a chilling realization: if terrorists did manage to smuggle a nuclear weapon into the city, there was almost nothing anyone could do about it.

In the days after September 11, doomsday scenarios like a nuclear attack on Manhattan suddenly seemed plausible. But during the six months that followed, as the U.S. struck back and the anthrax scare petered out and the fires at Ground Zero finally died down, the national nightmare about another calamitous terrorist strike went away.

The terrorists did not. Counterterrorism experts and government officials interviewed by *Time* say that for all the relative calm since September 11, America's luck will probably run out again, sooner or later. "It's going to be worse, and a lot of people are going to die," warns a U.S. counterterrorism official. "I don't think there's a damn thing we're going to be able to do about it." The government is so certain of another attack that it has assigned 100 civilian government officials to 24-hour rotations in underground bunkers, in a program that became known . . . as the "shadow government," ready to take the reins if the next megaterror target turns out to be Washington. Pentagon strategists say that even with al-Qaeda's [the terrorist cell that U.S. officials claim is responsible for the September 11 attacks] ranks scattered and its leaders in hiding, operatives around the world are primed and preparing to strike again. "If you're throwing enough darts at a board, eventually you're going to get something through," says a Pentagon strategist. "That's the way al-Qaeda looks at it."

The CIA and the nation's other intelligence bureaucracy were caught flat-footed by the September 11 attack.

Thousands of al-Qaeda terrorists survived the U.S. military assault in Afghanistan and are beginning to regroup. [In March 2001], U.S. forces attacked some 500 Taliban [the Afghanistan regime that was harboring terrorist Osama bin Laden] and al-Qaeda fighters holed up in the rugged, icy mountains outside the eastern town of Gardez, near the Pakistani border. The targets: four al-Qaeda training camps that were bombed [in 2001], but sources tell *Time* have since been reoccupied by al-Qaeda. . . . Locals say groups of armed men have moved into the area from the Pakistani border town of Miren-Shah. The latest battle involved at least 1,000 Afghan troops and 60 U.S. Special Forces, who advanced on an al-Qaeda encampment by taking control of roads around Shah-e-Kot. The lead forces were rebuffed by heavily armed al-Qaeda and Taliban fighters. U.S. aircraft, including B-52s, F-15Es, F-18s and AC-130 gunships, were called in to fire at enemy positions. At least one American was killed by hostile fire. "This could go on for several days," a Pentagon official said.

The CIA's failure to learn of the September 11 plot stemmed in large part from the CIA's inability to gather human intelligence about foreign threats.

As *Time* reported in January [2002], Western intelligence officials believe that al-Qaeda may now be under the control of Abu Zubaydah, a peripatetic aide of Osama bin Laden's who has run training camps in Afghanistan and coordinated terror cells in Europe and North America. A European terrorism expert says Zubaydah oversaw the training of 3,000 to 4,000 recruits in al-Qaeda terrorist camps, most of whom are "out there somewhere in the world right now." Zubaydah has instructed operatives to shave their beards, adopt Western clothing and "do whatever it takes to avoid detection and see their missions through," the expert says.

[Since September 2001], the Administration and Congress have mobilized massive amounts of government money, intelligence and personnel to track terrorists at home and abroad and tighten the country's protective net. But all nets have holes. A *Time* investigation found some good news—notably that the CIA, FBI and other intelligence and law-enforcement agencies are finally starting to work as a team. But in other critical areas, such as gathering and analyzing intelligence, strengthening homeland security and rounding up al-Qaeda, the U.S. has yet to solve its most grievous problems. Much of the more than $1 billion that Washington has poured into intelligence services since 9/11 is merely high-octane fuel flooding a leaky and misfiring engine. America's national security system is designed to fight Soviets rather than suicide bombers. Sources in the Pentagon, White House and Congress grumble that the CIA and the nation's other intelligence bureaucracy were caught flat-footed by the September 11 attack—"It was an abject intelligence failure," a White House aide says—and many still doubt that the U.S. intelligence community is capable of seeing the next one coming.

Experts warn about mass contamination of the nation's food supply and nuclear attacks on major U.S. cities precisely because these remote threats are the ones for which adequate defenses are not yet in place. The Coast Guard is arming itself against a possible terrorist attempt to destroy a major U.S. coastal city by detonating a tanker loaded with liquefied natural gas. The Bush Administration is bracing for another disaster. "We're as vulnerable today as we were on 9/10 or 9/12," says presidential counselor Karen Hughes. "We just know more." Here is what *Time* has learned about America's vulnerabilities—and how the U.S. is working to bolster its defenses on four crucial fronts.

Learning to spy again

Since September 11, no criticism of the CIA has been more damning than the fact that the agency's legions of highly trained spooks were less successful at infiltrating al-Qaeda than was a Marin County, California, 19-year-old named John Walker Lindh [who joined Taliban and al-Qaeda fighters to kill U.S. soldiers]. "They didn't see it; they didn't analyze it; they didn't locate it or disrupt it," says a U.S. official. "It's just that simple." In Senate hearings [in February 2002], CIA Director George Tenet, a Clinton Administration holdover who managed to hold on to his job after 9/11 because he is close to George W. Bush, stubbornly defended the agency's record. "It was not the result of the failure of attention and discipline and consistent effort," he insisted.

And yet intelligence officials acknowledge privately that September 11 laid bare many of the agency's most crippling weaknesses. Six months later, the problems remain—buried under billions of dollars in post-9/11 funding and stubbornly resistant to change. Insiders agree that the CIA's failure to learn of the September 11 plot stemmed in large part from the CIA's inability to gather human intelligence about foreign threats. The agency, a senior Administration official concedes, "got out of the human intelligence business in favor of technical collection" after the fall of the Soviet Union. Today the average overseas assignment for an agency spy-handler is three years, barely enough time to learn one's way around, let alone penetrate a terror cell. And with the passing of the Soviet threat, many CIA officials lost interest in doing dirty human espionage—which means recruiting dangerous characters who can act as spies and infiltrate terror networks such as al-Qaeda's. And even when informants were coaxed into cooperating, the CIA still required almost all "fully recruited" spies to take a polygraph test, something that scares off useful sources and in the past has failed to catch double agents. "We recruited a whole bunch of bad agents," admits a senior intelligence official. "We wasted a lot of taxpayer money that way."

Why does the CIA persist in spying the wrong way?

The CIA is larded with Russian specialists left over from the cold war, even as the agency struggles to recruit and train officers with proficiency in other tongues. In [2001's] graduating class of case officers, just 20% had usable skills in non-Romance languages. When the war in Afghanistan began, the CIA had only one Afghan analyst. . . . American intelligence agents in Kabul almost blew the chance to question a top-ranking Taliban minister, who may have had information on the hiding place of [Taliban leader] Mullah Omar. The spooks had yet to hire a Dari translator.

In response to *Time*'s questions about these shortcomings, two senior intelligence officials said the agency has worked hard to close the language gap and improve recruitment of informants. Since 1998, Tenet has instructed the CIA's espionage arm, the Directorate of Operations, to push its officers to diversify their language skills, boost recruitment and take greater risks. But despite some progress, a senior official admits, "we're not there yet." Robert Baer, a former CIA field operative in India, Tajikistan, Lebanon and Iraq, says the reforms did nothing to "break the cold war mold—it's all about the culture." The Administration has recalled old CIA hands with experience in Central Asia. Says an Administration official: "You ended up going back to retirees because the bench was so light on Afghanistan. We're still trying to get up to speed."

The dearth of qualified intelligence officers on the ground in Afghanistan has forced the U.S. to count on unreliable sources, dramatically increasing the risk of military mistakes, impeding the hunt for al-Qaeda leaders and giving Omar, bin Laden and their henchmen time to slip away. "The U.S. is totally dependent on locals, who have their own agenda," says an expert in the region. A senior intelligence official disputes the scope of the problem, telling *Time* that "this institution has never produced better human intelligence than it does today—but that doesn't mean that we don't need to do more."

The broad ground rules that gave each intelligence bureaucracy its own role and swath of territory don't make much sense in the new war.

Even when America sets its own agenda, there are serious problems. The U.S. spends more than 90% of its $35 billion annual intelligence budget on spying gadgetry rather than on gathering human intelligence, and most of that money goes not to the CIA but to spy agencies within the Department of Defense, such as the National Security Agency (which does eavesdropping and code breaking) and the National Reconnaissance Office (which flies imagery satellites). The priciest gadgets are not always the ones suited to fighting the terrorist threat. During the past five years, while the U.S. spent billions of dollars to build and launch about half a dozen radar-imaging spy satellites, the CIA and others built 60 Predator unmanned aerial vehicles (UAVS) at about $3 million apiece. The Predators, not the satellites, killed terrorists in Afghanistan.

High-tech surveillance can do little to track adversaries like the September 11 hijackers, especially if they are in the U.S. legally and careful about what they say on the phone. So why does the CIA persist in spying the wrong way? Part of the answer lies in the culture of secrecy that arose during the Cold War and continues to rule the agency's hearts and minds. Today the secrets the CIA needs to pick up are often easily accessible—such as the travel plans of the September 11 hijackers, two of whom managed to pay for their airline tickets with credit cards in their own names, even though the CIA had placed them on the terrorist watch list weeks before. Exploiting such "open sources" by combining them with newly discovered secrets is critical to fighting terrorists and others who hide in plain sight. And yet for years the agency discounted the value of open sources and let slip the quality of the intelligence analysts charged with studying them.

U.S. intelligence officials remain blind to this deficiency. Tenet insists that the agency's proper focus remains "the relentless pursuit of the secret." As long as U.S. intelligence continues to peer only in dark corners, we may struggle to discover what terrorists are hatching right in our backyard.

Share and share alike

Here's how the war on terrorism is supposed to work. In January 2002, a U.S. soldier prowling through an al-Qaeda compound in Afghanistan came across a document that contained outlines of a possible plot against the U.S. embassy in Sanaa, Yemen. The document contained the name of Fawaz Yahya al-Rabeei, a Saudi-born Yemeni who belonged to al-Qaeda, and it was passed to the CIA and FBI. Working with foreign intelligence services, the agencies came up with the names of 16 Rabeei associates and photographs of 13 of them. Then an FBI investigator poring over the list realized that the brother of one of the men was in U.S. custody in Guantanamo Bay, Cuba. On February 11 agents detailed to Camp X-Ray showed the prisoner the photos and persuaded him to talk. The prisoner told them that a terrorist attack—against U.S. installations in Yemen or even the U.S. itself—was planned for the next day.

At 9 that night—after consulting with intelligence officials, White House aides and Office of Homeland Security Director Tom Ridge—FBI Director Robert Mueller posted the names of the suspects and their mug shots on the FBI website and issued the government's most specific terror warning since September 11. No attack took place, but two days later a suspected al-Qaeda operative named Sameer Muhammad Ahmed al-Hada blew himself up with a hand grenade in a suburb of Sanaa, while fleeing from police. Al-Hada was connected to trouble: his brother-in-law is wanted by Yemeni police for conspiring in the September 11 hijackings, and another sister is married to Mustafa Abdul Kader al-Ansari, one of the 17 men the FBI believed had plans to attack America.

The Yemen case was a rare, real-time example of resourceful gumshoeing, timely intelligence and open communication among government agencies. The latter in particular went wanting in the days before September 11. Most notable is the story of Khalid al-Midhar. In January 2000 a group of al-Qaeda operatives met in Kuala Lumpur, Malaysia, to plot the attack on the U.S.S. Cole. Malaysian authorities caught the meeting on a surveillance videotape and turned it over to the CIA. Last summer the agency identified one of the attendees as al-Midhar, a Saudi who intelligence officials thought had entered the U.S. shortly after the meeting in Malaysia and left six months later. The CIA put his name on a watch list and handed it over to the Immigration and Naturalization Service—but by then al-Midhar had slipped back into the U.S. Within the next few days, the CIA briefed the FBI on al-Midhar. FBI officials say they initiated a frantic manhunt for al-Midhar but never found him. On September 11, authorities believe, he flew American Airlines flight 77 into the Pentagon. Al-Midhar bought his September 11 airline ticket under his own name, but American Airlines officials say no government authorities informed them he was on a terrorism watch list.

That Al-Midhar could elude three federal agencies, all of which knew his identity and the danger he posed, highlights the lack of coordination among U.S. intelligence agencies, whose biggest problem may be the intelligence system's splintered structure. The array of semiautonomous agencies—13 in all—share a secure computer network, but collaboration is not in their nature. Interaction between outsiders and CIA analysts or officials is difficult. Says a frustrated Administration official: "We don't have a place where it all comes together."

The broad ground rules that gave each intelligence bureaucracy its own role and swath of territory don't make much sense in the new war. The CIA has largely stayed out of domestic intelligence gathering, in part because of limits set by Congress in the '70s to protect citizens from the agency's excesses, such as dosing unwitting subjects with LSD. During the cold war and afterward, the Pentagon, FBI and CIA split the responsibility for tracking foreign threats, but each agency kept the others in the dark about what it was doing. That division of labor failed completely in spotting clues to September 11, so it's good news that in the race to stop the next attack, the lines between fiefs have finally started to blur. The September 11 terrorists crossed national boundaries at will. In response, more FBI agents are working overseas than ever before. The [USA] Patriot Act passed in October 2001, gives the CIA greater access to law-enforcement information and allows the National Security Agency to obtain warrants more easily for domestic wiretaps. In Afghanistan, the CIA has unleashed its 150-man covert paramilitary force to conduct sabotage, collect intelligence and train Northern Alliance guerrillas.

Once intelligence has been collected, analyzed and shared, it must be acted on.

The paragon of interagency cooperation is the CIA's Counterterrorism Center [CTC], which was created in 1986 as a way to get FBI and CIA agents working side by side. In the past three years, the CTC has broken up three planned attacks by the Hizbollah terror group outside the Middle East, all of them targeting locations where Americans could have been killed. The CTC is everything the rest of the intelligence community is not: coordinated, dynamic and designed for the post–cold war threat. As a result, its staff has doubled to 1,000 since September 11, and the Administration has deluged the center with new funding.

But the CTC's staffers make up just 1% of the U.S. intelligence community. Some critics say the only sensible reform is for the CTC to become a model for the larger community—merging multiple intelligence agencies under the authority of the director of Central Intelligence. Congressional sources tell *Time* that an advisory panel headed by former National Security Adviser Brent Scowcroft will recommend just such a reorganization later this year [2002]. But the idea probably won't go anywhere. Defense Secretary Donald Rumsfeld is expected to oppose any proposal to take away the Pentagon's control over the Defense Department's intelligence agencies, where most intelligence dollars go. Tenet, who spent 10 years as a staffer on Capitol Hill, doesn't want to challenge Rumsfeld, who is at the height of his power. Those who know Tenet say he has little taste for taking on superiors. "[Tenet's] focus is always just going to be on getting the job done," says a source close to the Scowcroft panel.

A better shield

Once intelligence has been collected, analyzed and shared, it must be acted on—used to set priorities and bolster defenses. The government knows it can't wait. In the past six months, billions have already gone toward reinforcing cockpit doors, tightening the airline baggage-screening process and hiring 28,000 new federal employees at airports to replace the private security firms that let al-Qaeda through on September 11. In October [2001] the Administration created a new Office of Homeland Security to deal exclusively with the job of preparing the country for future terrorist threats. Since he took the job of Homeland Security czar, former Pennsylvania Governor Tom Ridge has had some rough sledding; Bush gave him no authority over Cabinet members or agencies, which means he lacks the clout to win crucial bureaucratic fights. But Ridge has shown his skill in the Washington art of writing checks. The Administration's $38 billion homeland-security budget proposes a $380 million system to track the entry and exit of noncitizens and gives $282 million to the Coast Guard for protecting ports and coastal areas. This week [of March 11, 2002], sources tell *Time*, Ridge's office plans to announce a new color-coded alert system to warn local law enforcement and the public about threats within U.S. borders. Even the military is setting up a new bureaucracy, the U.S. Northern Command, dedicated to defending the homeland. By October 1, [2002,] the military hopes to put a four-star general in charge of a standing domestic military force devoted to flying combat air patrols, guarding the borders and responding to attacks on U.S. soil.

Terrorists aren't likely to be deterred. There's plenty of intelligence that al-Qaeda operatives want to bring down more airliners—witness Richard Reid [who allegedly tried to blow up a plane using bombs hidden in his shoes]—and the government is still trying to get serious about stopping them. As recently as last month, Transportation Department investigators succeeded in slipping weapons and explosives past screening personnel and onto an aircraft at Miami International Airport.

Thanks to the new airport-security bill passed in Congress last November [2001], airline security has been taken out of the hands of the FAA [Federal Aviation Administration] and given to the newly created federal Transportation Security Administration (TSA). But many of the changes that were supposed to be carried out by the TSA either haven't been implemented or have been killed by compromise. Federal baggage screeners are in place at only 15 of the country's 429 airports, and the TSA has not yet bought the 2,000 large detection devices it aims to have operating within nine months to inspect checked baggage for explosives. Airlines still aren't required to match bags to passengers on every plane; on some aircraft, the improvements to cockpit doors amount to nothing but "a silly little bar," in the words of one pilot. "It's easy to imagine hundreds of horrific possibilities," says TSA deputy head Steven McHale. "We can become paralyzed if we start thinking about all possible threats."

In countless other areas as well, homeland security still needs an upgrade. The Administration plans to hire 800 more customs agents to police the borders but still lacks a system for tracking whether immigrants who enter legally overstay their visas, which three of the September 11 hijackers did. Ridge . . . has proposed the sensible reform of getting the various border-control agencies—Customs, [Immigration and Naturalization Service], Border Patrol and Coast Guard—to operate under a single command and work off the same technology. But he lacks the power to make it happen. Despite calls for the Federal Government to improve security at the country's nuclear power plants and weapons sites—and the chilling discovery in Afghanistan of evidence that al-Qaeda may try to target them—little has been done to lock down the sites or to clear the air corridors above them. In October [2001] the FAA briefly banned aircraft from flying below 18,000 ft. and within 10 miles of 86 sensitive sites, including several nuclear power plants, but the ban was lifted in November and has not been reinstated.

The single most effective strategy for pre-empting another attack is to hit the attackers first.

Government agencies are starting to prepare for other previously unimaginable threats. Experts meeting in Lenox, Massachussetts, said hackers in the Middle East have probed the huge computers that control the nation's electric-power grid, and the government has received reports of possible physical reconnaissance of power plants by terrorists. Republican Senator Jon Kyl frets about explosives, such as the three substances found in Reid's shoes, which in small quantities might be missed by airport screening devices and some bomb-sniffing dogs. Small amounts of old-fashioned explosives are potent enough to blow a hole in a fuselage, and experts can't say for certain whether airport detectors can spot them. "I don't really want to talk about this publicly," Kyl says, "but it remains difficult to do something about."

The homeland-security budget is aimed at keeping casualties down; almost all of the $9.5 billion allocated to combat bioterrorism, for instance, goes toward training and equipping local public-health authorities to treat victims and haul out bodies in the event of an attack. The assumption, of course, is that an attack will come. "We need to accept that the possibility of terrorism is a permanent condition for the foreseeable future," Ridge told *Time*. "We just have to accept it."

Catching bad guys

The single most effective strategy for pre-empting another attack is to hit the attackers first—to disrupt and root out the terrorists who are planning the next strike. That's hard but not impossible. The September 11 hijackers kept low profiles, for example, but didn't plan the attacks in cloistered secrecy. Mohammed Atta and his crew received money from al-Qaeda paymasters through traceable banking channels. Nine of them were singled out for special airport-security screenings on the morning of the attacks, the *Washington Post* reported, yet managed to slip through. The two hijackers who were on the government terrorist watch list before September 11 possessed valid driver's licenses under their own names and paid for their tickets with credit cards that the FBI could have easily tracked. In some cases, the FBI failed to share information it possessed on suspect individuals with other law-enforcement authorities; in others, the feds simply didn't pay close enough attention.

They do now. Since September 11, the number of FBI personnel working on counterterrorism has grown from 1,000 to 4,000. A new cybercrime division monitors credit-card-fraud schemes that terrorists use to fund their activities. Stung by criticism over its historic reluctance to share secret evidence with local cops, the FBI now sees it doesn't have a choice. Edward Flynn, the police chief in Arlington County, Virginia, says the FBI is giving local cops more leads than they can handle. "They feel compelled to tell us this stuff," he says.

Meanwhile, arrests of al-Qaeda suspects in the U.S. have dwindled. A handful of people in federal custody are still being investigated for possible links to terrorist activity. The worldwide dragnet has snared 600 alleged al-Qaeda operatives. And yet the bottom line is sobering: after six months of gumshoe work by just about every law-enforcement official in the U.S., the number of al-Qaeda sleeper cells that have been busted inside the country is precisely zero. Does that mean bin Laden's men have gone further underground? "We don't know," says an FBI official. "If you go back and look at the hijackers, they had zero contact with any known al-Qaeda people we were looking at. They didn't break laws. They didn't do anything to come to anybody's attention. Are there other people in the U.S. like that? We don't know."

As long as such uncertainty persists, so will the military assault on al-Qaeda abroad. The U.S. military campaign has removed bin Laden's sanctuary and degraded his infrastructure of terror. Pentagon sources say that the U.S. has killed as many as eight high-ranking al-Qaeda officials, but most of the 11,000 terrorists believed to have spent time in al-Qaeda camps are still on the loose. Efforts to apprehend al-Qaeda fighters in Afghanistan have slowed, as thousands have bought safe refuge in the hamlets and villages of the Afghan countryside. "The mission is to take al-Qaeda apart piece by piece," says Mohammed Anwar, the head of intelligence in Mazar-i-Sharif. "But it's very difficult work." CIA, FBI and military intelligence officials have spent eight weeks interviewing the 300 detainees in Cuba for information on the whereabouts of the al-Qaeda leadership, but defense sources told *Time* that any prisoners now in U.S. custody know little, if anything, about bin Laden's coordinates. While there is a genuine debate inside the government about whether he is still alive, there is far less argument about what will happen after Washington is able to confirm that he is dead. A U.S. official told *Time* last week that it is widely presumed that al-Qaeda sleeper cells will take retaliatory action once the terrorist leader is killed or proved dead.

With al-Qaeda sprinkled around the globe, it becomes harder to develop the intelligence needed to take the fight to the enemy. [In March 2002,] the Administration gave its clearest signal yet that the war won't stop in Afghanistan or even the Philippines, when it announced plans to send special-ops troops to Yemen and the former Soviet republic of Georgia, both countries where al-Qaeda fighters are believed to be hiding.

By keeping the pressure up, the U.S. hopes to correct its biggest mistake of all. According to this view, the U.S.'s failure to retaliate massively after past al-Qaeda attacks against U.S. military barracks, battleships and embassies tempted bin Laden to go after ever more outrageous targets—and finally the World Trade Center. Now the U.S. has destroyed al-Qaeda's training camps and undermined bin Laden's capacity to lead. And yet the September 11 hijackings were years in the making—which means bin Laden could have ordered up another, more lethal attack before his world came apart. "We were overwhelmingly defensive in our orientation before September 11," Admiral Dennis Blair, the head of the U.S.'s Pacific Command, told *Time*. "Now we've gone on the offensive." The big question is whether we did so in time.

2

The CIA Cannot Be Blamed for the Terrorist Attacks on America

Thomas Houlahan

Thomas Houlahan is director of the Military Assessment Program of the William R. Nelson Institute at James Madison University.

The CIA is not at fault for the intelligence failure that led to the September 11, 2001, terrorist attacks on America. Rather, the administrations of Bill Clinton and George W. Bush are to blame. These administrations set intelligence priorities for the CIA, and both told the agency to focus its attention on China, which they considered the most serious threat to the United States. By focusing on China, however, the CIA ignored Islamic terrorists such as Osama bin Laden, who has been named as the man behind the September 11 attacks.

Almost as soon as the shock of the [September 11, 2001, terrorist attacks on America] wore off, questions were raised about how such an attack could have happened, and blame began to be apportioned. One of the chief targets of blame was the CIA.

Over a period of anywhere from one to three years, a sophisticated terrorist plan had been hatched. Leaders had been chosen and men had been trained for its implementation.

Yet, for all of its resources, at no point had the CIA gotten wind of any of it. The agency, it seemed, had a lot to answer for.

I believe that the CIA cannot be blamed for this disaster. Many present and former CIA agents claimed that meddling politicians overly concerned with propriety were at fault. Strict rules had been promulgated regarding the types of people that the CIA was allowed to employ as sources. As a result, the agency was forbidden to deal with the truly nasty people that its agents felt they needed to cultivate to get close to the center of terrorist conspiracies. Because of this, according to these agents, the value of the CIA's "human intelligence" suffered.

From "Commentary: The CIA and September 11," by Thomas Houlahan, *United Press International*, January 30, 2002. Copyright © 2002 by United Press International. Reprinted with permission.

This misses the point. It is true that political leaders had been concerned that it was inappropriate for men with serious blood on their hands to be on the payroll of the world's leading democracy. However, the main problem was that such "assets" had often proven not only embarrassing, but also worthless. "Intelligence" from deeply unscrupulous people is inherently unreliable, and too often such sources turn out to be double agents. Too often the information they provide turns out to be disinformation. As a former officer in the Army's 82nd Airborne Division, I can tell you that the intelligence we got back in the glory days of human intelligence wasn't very reliable. The CIA is probably better off under the stricter rules.

Looking in the wrong direction

The real problem was mainly that in previous years, the CIA had been looking in the wrong direction in terms of threat assessment. Though President Bill Clinton gave lip service to the fight against terrorism, it was never translated into action. There would be small spasms of activity after a terrorist act, but that was about it. As an analyst in a think tank that specializes in terrorism, I was shocked at how little government interest there was in the subject before September 11.

The CIA looked in the direction it was told to look.

As far as the United States government was concerned, China was the threat, even though there was not a single Chinese military base outside China and no competent military analyst believed that China was anywhere near capable of seizing Taiwan. The focus on China intensified after the Bush administration took office and the so-called "Blue Team," a group of anti-China hardliners, were calling the foreign policy shots.

In those days, if you were a military analyst and you didn't see China as a major military threat, you were regarded as either naive or unpatriotic. Either way, you had no place in the national defense discussion.

Suspicion of China intensified still further when, on April 1, 2001, a U.S. Navy E-3 surveillance plane collided with a Chinese interceptor and was forced to land on Hainan Island. The crew was released after 11 days of tension between the United States and China.

A few analysts were concerned that the United States government was unduly concerned with China and was treating the threat of terrorism rather lightly. A few days after China released the Navy crew (almost five months before September 11), I wrote:

> "Immediately after the Pakistani Army assumed control of Pakistan, the United States government decided that it was necessary to basically break off relations with Pakistan to teach her military a lesson. The government did this, knowing that, among other things, in breaking off relations with Pakistan, we would lose our ability to keep international terrorist mastermind Osama bin Laden (headquartered in neighboring Afghanistan) under effective surveillance. Still,

> the government did it, without batting an eyelash. So, let me get this straight. The government is willing to blind itself with regard to one of the world's most dangerous terrorists and risk having truck bombs go off in lower Manhattan to teach the Pakistani military a lesson. No problem there. However, the government can't possibly scale back surveillance flights around a quiet island, nowhere near Taiwan, governed by a nation with whom relations have been cordial for quite some time in the interests of continued cordial relations with that nation (which is also the major regional military power). That would be too risky. That would be a threat to national security. What sense does that make?"

I should add that fear of China had undoubtedly been a major motivating factor in the Clinton administration's decision to distance itself from Pakistan. The claim that the United States government did not feel comfortable dealing with the [Pakistani president Pervez] Musharraf government because it was undemocratic really doesn't stand up well to scrutiny.

Kuwait, Saudi Arabia and Egypt are hardly Jeffersonian democracies, yet the government shows no apparent discomfort in dealing with these nations. The United States also had no trouble dealing with Pakistan's last military leader, Gen. Mohammed Zia ul-Haq, a much harsher ruler than Musharraf. I believe that the decision had more to do with Pakistan's friendly relations with China and a craving for closer U.S. ties with India, a country that anti-China hawks covet as a counterweight to China.

As the events of September 11 have demonstrated, while the CIA's attention was focused on China, bin Laden was planning his greatest terrorist outrage. It was not the CIA's fault, however. The CIA serves the United States government. It doesn't set its priorities, each presidential administration does. The CIA looked in the direction it was told to look.

The blame, in my opinion, belongs to the officials who ordered it to look in the wrong direction. In short, I am saying that many of the figures who have become media superstars due to the success of the war in Afghanistan and their predecessors in the Clinton administration are the ones with a lot to answer for.

3

The CIA Should Be Granted Expanded Powers to Fight Terrorism

Rich Galen

Rich Galen, former press secretary to Representatives Dan Quayle and Newt Gingrich, has had articles published in most major newspapers and has been a frequent guest on television news shows.

Expanding the CIA's powers to fight terrorism by passing the USA-PATRIOT Act does not constitute an intolerable suspension of personal liberties. On the contrary, in times of national emergency, certain civil liberties must be sacrificed to ensure the common good. Most Americans agree that the CIA should be given the information-sharing capabilities it needs to fight terrorism. In the wake of the September 11, 2001, terrorist attacks on America, Americans have accepted the need to sacrifice some personal liberties in exchange for greater security.

Editor's note: The USA-PATRIOT Act was passed into law in October 2001.

[In the days following the September 11, 2001, terrorist attacks on America,] Attorney General John Ashcroft has been on Capitol Hill trying to convince the Congress to grant enhanced powers to the FBI, the CIA and assorted other agencies opposed to villainy, to find terrorists and bring them to justice before they can carry out their wicked work.

A major feature of the new legislation [USA-PATRIOT Act] has to do with detaining, for an indeterminate amount of time, non-US citizens who are accused of being terrorists.

Another part of the bill would allow law enforcement agencies to get permission to intercept communications by targeting the individual they want to tap, rather than the specific gadget that person will be using, as is (more or less) the case now.

On MSNBC, [moderator] Dan Abrams tried to get me and Julian Ep-

From "Find Them," by Rich Galen, www.mullings.com, September 26, 2001. Copyright © 2001 by Rich Galen. Reprinted with permission.

stein to either disagree with each other (which we did not do) about whether this was an intolerable suspension of personal liberties; or agree with him (which we also did not do) that this was an intolerable suspension of personal liberties.

In times of war—and for the duration of the emergency—certain civil liberties must give way to the needs of the common good.

Dan said that the bill would allow the government to put non-US citizens away for 10 or 15 years without any access to a court. I said he was making it sound like a scene from [the play] *Les Miserables* [that portrays a man condemned to prison for stealing a loaf of bread]. Julian who, until recently, was the Democratic staff director of the House Judiciary Committee, said that the government already has the power to deport people using secret evidence which might NEVER be divulged to the defendant.

Balancing civil liberties with the common good

The Constitution of the United States has always had a certain amount of elasticity depending upon the specific needs of the period. Abraham Lincoln suspended habeas corpus during the civil war. The internment of Japanese-Americans during World War II is well documented and appropriately regretted.

In times of war—and for the duration of the emergency—certain civil liberties must give way to the needs of the common good. At its most basic level, the protections of the criminal justice system are completely suspended on a battlefield: Individual soldiers are granted the powers of police, prosecutor, judge, jury, and executioner.

Many of the people who have traveled by air since the resumption of commercial service have been aghast at the LACK of additional security evident at airports. People are going to the airport hours in advance and are willing—eager—to be subjected to a much more rigorous screening process than they would have put up with previously.

When the only additional security procedure seems to be having to show your picture ID at the x-ray machine, it doesn't seem like enough.

Similarly, if the FBI, the CIA, the Drug Enforcement Administration (DEA), the Immigration and Naturalization Service (INS), and the other groups responsible for our safety say they need to—at a minimum—be able to talk to each other and share information, most of us are willing to let them have at it.

Before September 11, 2001, there were many of us who were in something of a lather about the notion of having our faces scanned by a hidden camera, compared to a database, and authorities alerted to our presence.

Today, it doesn't seem like that bad an idea.

Before September 11, the notion of having to present not just a picture ID, but maybe something with my fingerprints or retinal pattern to get on an airplane would have been fodder for a long (and possibly somewhat amusing) rant.

Today, it doesn't seem like such a bad idea, either.

There are a number of people in their 50's who are comparing this situation with the days of anti-war activities during the Viet Nam era when government agencies—notably the FBI—kept files on people for exercising their First Amendment rights.

No thinking person is in favor of stifling legitimate dissent. But no thinking person should confuse this era with that.

The House and the Senate will mark up [the USA-PATRIOT bill] granting most of the expanded powers to locate and disable terrorists that the Administration is asking for.

Because it is what most of the American population is asking for.

4

The CIA Should Not Be Granted Expanded Powers to Fight Terrorism

American Civil Liberties Union

The American Civil Liberties Union is the nation's oldest and largest civil liberties organization.

In the wake of the September 11, 2001, terrorist attacks on America, Congress passed the USA-PATRIOT Act, which grants the CIA expanded powers to fight terrorism. This act allows the CIA to spy on Americans by permitting a vast array of domestic information gathering from school records, Internet activity, and telephone conversations. The act removes the safeguards established by the Church Committee in the 1970s, which curtailed the CIA's domestic intelligence gathering activities in order to protect Americans. One of the most serious dangers inherent in the act is the requirement that law enforcement officers share with the CIA foreign intelligence information obtained in the United States. However, much of this information sharing is not necessary to protect against terrorist attacks and constitutes a violation of Americans' civil rights.

The final version of the anti-terrorism legislation [enacted in response to the September 11, 2001, terrorist attacks on America], the Uniting and Strengthening America By Providing Appropriate Tools Required To Intercept and Obstruct Terrorism (H.R. 3162, the "USA-PATRIOT Act,") puts the Central Intelligence Agency back in the business of spying on Americans.[1] It permits a vast array of information gathering on U.S. citizens from school records, financial transactions, Internet activity, telephone conversations, information gleaned from grand jury proceedings and criminal investigations to be shared with the CIA (and other non-law enforcement officials) even if it pertains to Americans. The information

1. The USA-PATRIOT Act was signed into law by President George W. Bush on October 26, 2001.

From "How the USA-PATRIOT Act Puts the CIA Back in the Business of Spying on Americans," www.aclu.org, 2001. Copyright © 2001 by the American Civil Liberties Union. Reprinted with permission.

would be shared without a court order. The bill also gives the Director of the Central Intelligence Agency, acting in his capacity as head of the Intelligence Community, enormous power to manage the collection and dissemination of intelligence information gathered in the U.S. This new authority supercedes existing guidelines issued to protect Americans from unwarranted surveillance by U.S. agencies such as the FBI.

To appreciate the dangers of the USA-PATRIOT Act, we should take a moment to revisit one of the shameful chapters in recent history that led to restrictions on the CIA.

The Church Committee

Until the mid-1970's, both the CIA and the National Security Agency (NSA) illegally investigated Americans. Despite the statutory provision in its charter prohibiting the CIA from engaging in law enforcement or internal security functions, the CIA spied on as many as seven thousand Americans in Operation CHAOS. This operation in the 1960's and early 1970's involved spying on people who opposed the war in Vietnam, or who were student activists or were so-called black nationalists. Operation CHAOS involved an extensive program of information sharing from the FBI and other agencies to the CIA. The CIA received all of the FBI's reports on the American peace movement, which numbered over 1,000/month by June of 1970, according to a Senate report issued by the Senate Select Committee to Study Governmental Operations With Respect To Intelligence Activities (Church Committee Report). The Church Committee Report revealed how simple passive information sharing from other agencies to the CIA became authorized spying and data collection on lawful American political activity protected by the First Amendment. Once CIA officials expressed interest in particular types of information on American individuals and groups, other federal and local agencies were persuaded to covertly spy on citizens at the CIA's behest. The Church Committee reported:

> The mechanics of the CHAOS operation, both in performing the mission undertaken by the CIA and in servicing the FBI's needs, involved the establishment of files and retention of information on thousands of Americans.
>
> To the extent that [the] information related to domestic activity, its maintenance by the CIA, although perhaps not itself the performance of an internal security function, is a step toward the dangers of a domestic secret police against which the prohibition of the charter sought to guard.

After these abuses were exposed, the CIA's domestic surveillance activities and collection of information about Americans were greatly curtailed. For example, the Foreign Intelligence Surveillance Act made it clear that the Department of Justice would have the leading role in gathering foreign intelligence in the United States. The USA-PATRIOT Act would tear down these safeguards and once again permit the CIA to create dossiers on constitutionally protected activities of Americans and eliminate judicial review of such practices.

Eviscerating the "necessity requirement"

The "USA-PATRIOT Act" permits the wide sharing of sensitive information gathered in criminal investigations by law enforcement agencies with intelligence agencies including the CIA and the NSA, and other federal agencies including the INS, Secret Service, and Department of Defense.

For example, Section 203(a) of the bill would permit law enforcement agents to provide to the CIA foreign intelligence and counterintelligence information revealed to a grand jury. No court order would be required. In authorizing this flow of sensitive information, Section 203(a) would redefine "foreign intelligence information" for purposes of this section to permit more liberal sharing of information about U.S. persons—citizens and lawful permanent residents of the United States.

As a result, the foreign intelligence information about Americans that could be shared with the CIA need not be information that is necessary to protect against attacks, or is necessary to the national defense or security of the United States. This "necessity" requirement of the Foreign Intelligence Surveillance Act effectively operates to protect Americans from unwarranted surveillance for "intelligence" as opposed to criminal purposes. This requirement is eviscerated under the information sharing provisions of the USA-PATRIOT Act. In addition, the sharing of grand jury information authorized by Section 203(a) is not limited to information about the person being investigated. Thus, a witness called before the grand jury to provide evidence against the person being investigated, or about others, might be less forthcoming if it is known that the supposedly secret information could be shared with the CIA.

The USA-PATRIOT Act would . . . permit the CIA to create dossiers on constitutionally protected activities of Americans.

Section 203(b) would permit law enforcement officers to share with the CIA intercepts of telephone and Internet conversations. No court order would be necessary to authorize the sharing of this sensitive information. This section also broadens the definition of foreign intelligence information to include more information about Americans. It includes no meaningful restrictions on subsequent use of the recorded conversations. For example, there is nothing in the bill that prevents this information from being used to screen candidates who apply for government jobs. Also, Section 203(b) does not prohibit the CIA from sharing with foreign governments surveillance information gleaned from a criminal investigation, even if sharing that information could put at risk members of a person's family who live abroad.

Foreign intelligence information sharing

Section 203(d) broadly permits the sharing of any foreign intelligence or counterintelligence information obtained as part of a criminal investigation to be disclosed to the CIA and other intelligence, defense and immigration authorities. No court order would be required, and for purposes of this information sharing, "foreign intelligence information" would be re-defined to permit more sharing of information about Americans. Section 905 of the bill mandates disclosure to the CIA of foreign intelligence information obtained in connection with a criminal investigation, but this section does not re-define "foreign intelligence information." These proposals represent extraordinary extensions of the current authorities of the foreign intelligence agencies, including the CIA, to obtain information about Americans.

While some sharing of information may be appropriate in some limited circumstances, it should only be done with strict safeguards. These safeguards include protecting information about U.S. persons from disclosure to the CIA, requiring court approval for disclosure, limiting disclosure to foreign intelligence information as defined in the Foreign Intelligence Surveillance Act, limiting disclosure to foreign governments, and requiring that disclosed information be marked to indicate how it was obtained and how it can and cannot be used or disseminated. The bill lacks all of these safeguards. As a result it may lead to the very abuses that the Church Committee exposed decades ago.

The USA-PATRIOT Act would empower the Director of the Central Intelligence Agency (DCI) to establish the priorities for the collection and dissemination of intelligence information gathered in the U.S. He would exercise this power while acting in his capacity as head of the intelligence community. The Attorney General currently performs this function.

Though this provision includes language purporting to prohibit the DCI from directing or undertaking electronic surveillance operations, it includes no similar prohibition relating to physical searches for intelligence purposes. More importantly, Section 901 appears to contemplate that the DCI would be empowered to identify to the Department of Justice and to the FBI potential targets of intelligence surveillance in the United States, including particular people and groups to be surveilled. Such a power would be inherent to the ability to "establish requirements and priorities" for the collection of foreign intelligence information under the Foreign Intelligence Surveillance Act.

It amounts to a rather clear case of giving the CIA an enhanced role in domestic intelligence gathering—including the gathering of intelligence about United States citizens—in the U.S. It also runs directly contrary to the statutory prohibition in the CIA's charter barring it from engaging in internal security functions.

5

The Ban Against CIA Assassinations Should Be Amended

Richard Lowry

Richard Lowry is editor of the National Review.

The CIA should be permitted to assassinate leaders of nations with which the United States is at war. The ban on CIA assassinations, which was issued in 1976 by then-president Gerald Ford, was a wrong-headed decision made as a result of national guilt over the Vietnam War. The ban is not required by international laws governing war. In fact, it is lawful to employ any method used to kill enemy soldiers to kill an enemy leader. Targeted killings are also morally superior to other wartime policies such as all-out war, which harms more people than assassination, or economic sanctions, which harm civilians. The fact that the CIA has bungled some assassination attempts is no reason to ban targeted killings.

After Iraqi president Saddam Hussein invaded Kuwait in 1990, President George Bush signed a secret finding authorizing the CIA to attempt to overthrow the Iraqi dictator. Bob Woodward reports in his book *The Commanders* that "the CIA was not to violate the ban on involvement in assassination attempts, but rather recruit Iraqi dissidents to remove Saddam from power." In other words, according to the strict letter of the finding, Saddam was to be ousted not "dead or alive," but only alive—at least as far as the CIA had any control over it.

Around the same time, defense secretary Dick Cheney fired Air Force chief of staff Michael J. Dugan for telling reporters that the U.S. wanted to "decapitate" the Iraqi regime by killing Saddam and his family. Dugan was sacked not just for revealing operational details, Cheney explained, but also for speaking favorably about a policy that might violate the ban on assassinations. "We never talk about the targeting of specific individuals who are officials of other governments," Cheney said.

From "A View to a Kill: Assassination in War and Peace," by Richard Lowry, *National Review*, March 11, 2002. Copyright © 2002 by National Review, Inc. Reprinted with permission.

A moral hangover

Why this tender concern for Saddam Hussein's well-being? It was part of a hangover from the implosion of America's moral self-confidence that occurred in the 1970s, in the wake of Vietnam and the Church committee's battering of the CIA as a hapless, dirty-tricks operation.[1] The Ford administration, bowing to congressional pressure, rushed to issue an executive order banning assassination. During the Gulf War, the first Bush administration didn't let its regard for the Ford order actually stop it from bombing Saddam's personal compounds, but it pretended not to have entertained the idea of specifically killing him.

This garble reflects a lack of exactly the sort of clarity that the war on terrorism demands: Killing enemy belligerents, even if they are heads of state, is a lawful and moral application of American power. The Ford order on assassinations—reissued by Ronald Reagan as Executive Order 12333—should either be amended, or at the very least publicly reinterpreted, so there is no longer any confusion on this point. It is the right of the U.S. to target and kill individuals in the chain of command of a country with which we are formally, or as a practical matter, at war.

The upshot of the Church committee's work in 1975 was that after 30 years of the twilight struggle, the United States should get out of the twilight business. The Cold War consensus had been based on the idea that our enemy was evil and ruthless, and therefore we would have to employ rough means to defeat it (as a commission headed by Herbert Hoover put it starkly in 1954, "hitherto acceptable norms of human conduct do not apply").

It is the right of the U.S. to target and kill individuals in the chain of command of a country with which we are . . . at war.

The Church committee was devoted to the proposition that engaging in such nasty business made us no better—actually, somehow much worse—than the Soviets. "The committee was struck," said the Church report, "by the basic tension—if not incompatibility—of covert operations and the demands of the constitutional system." The U.S. should worry more about its virtue and less about power politics. "We need not be so frightened by each Russian intervention," Senator Frank Church said. "We have gained little, and lost a great deal, by our past policy of compulsive interventionism."

From this aloof perspective on world affairs, the committee concluded that "assassination is unacceptable in our society." Period. It dredged up stories of far-fetched attempts to off Cuban president Fidel Castro—poisoned cigars, poisoned diving suits—that made assassination seem a risible exercise (as if the fact that we were bad at assassination proved that we should never do it). It also focused on shadowy U.S. involvement in the killings in the 1950s and 1960s of Patrice Lumumba in Congo, Rafael Tru-

1. The Church committee investigated CIA involvement in planned or actual assassinations of foreign leaders in the 1970s.

jillo in the Dominican Republic, and Ngo Dinh Diem in Vietnam.

The committee had a point. There were questions about whether the CIA was operating with the necessary democratic accountability in the U.S., and these killings took place over what essentially amounted to peacetime political preferences (although peacetime was difficult to define in the Cold War, since the Soviets envisioned it as just another opportunity to wage war). So, these acts were more properly thought of as unlawful assassinations rather than legitimate wartime killings.

In judging such killings, as former Reagan and Bush official David Rivkin points out, this is really the crucial distinction: between peace and war. From the Romans to the U.N. Charter, international law has recognized certain "protected persons"—heads of state, diplomats—who can't be killed by a foreign power in peacetime. But, as Rivkin says, "war changes everything." There is a right under international law to target an enemy's command and control during wartime, including anyone in the chain of command right up to the head of state (especially when, as in the case of Saddam, he wears a uniform and a sidearm).

A historic leftover

Why, then, does such an odor still attach to targeting specific individuals in wartime? It is partly a leftover from 18th- and 19th-century rules of warfare, when battle was essentially an interruption of otherwise correct relations between fellow sovereigns. As Notre Dame law professor Gerard V. Bradley points out, it wouldn't have occurred to the French, for instance, to try to kill British prime minister William Pitt [who tried to defeat Napoleon's armies in 1804]. It just wasn't done. But this all changed with the advent of total war, and of leaders, such as Adolf Hitler, unfit for the chummy "community of nations."

In June 1943, the Germans shot down what they took to be British prime minister Winston Churchill's plane. Two months before, the Americans had shot down Japanese admiral Isoroku Yamamoto's plane, after an intelligence intercept revealed that he would be inspecting front-line Japanese bases. Admiral Chester Nimitz carefully considered whether any of Yamamoto's possible replacements would be worse—i.e., more talented or better liked by Japanese troops—and, after concluding they wouldn't, ordered the attack. No one at the time complained that this act was incompatible with American values.

Any method that is lawful for attacking an enemy army is also lawful as a way of killing an enemy leader.

The hesitation to endorse such targeted killings today—when we are a century and several million deaths beyond the age of international chivalry—involves a misunderstanding of what exactly is proscribed by international law. According to Article 23b of the Hague Convention, "It is especially forbidden to kill or wound treacherously individuals belonging to the hostile nation or army." This is not, however, a prohibition on all targeted killings. Instead, for a killing to be considered an unlawful assassination, it has to use treacherous means.

Treachery is an extremely narrow concept. In current practice, we seem, oddly, to interpret it as anything that would be too precise or sneaky. So, killing Saddam Hussein with a barrage of guided bombs, as long as we are not too frank about whether his death is intended or not, is acceptable (not treacherous), but killing him with one cruise missile aimed right at his bedroom, or, even worse, shooting him with a sniper team or setting a booby trap in front of his motorcade, is forbidden (treacherous). This from-15,000-feet rule is as irrational as it sounds.

As a terrorist bandit, [Osama] bin Laden enjoys the protection of no international conventions against assassination or anything else.

In fact, any method that is lawful for attacking an enemy army is also lawful as a way of killing an enemy leader. The use of perfidious means to take advantage of a target's trust—such as disguising a U.S. hit team as U.N. negotiators—is forbidden. (Saudi terrorist Osama bin Laden's use of assassins posing as journalists to kill Northern Alliance leader Ahmed Massoud is a classic case of perfidy.) Otherwise, there is nothing that says targeted killings must take place from the air. As the U.S. Army Memorandum of Law puts it, "No distinction is made between an attack accomplished by aircraft, missile, naval gunfire, artillery, mortar, infantry assault, ambush . . . booby trap, a single shot by a sniper, a commando attack, or other similar means."

Assassination is morally and practically justified

International law aside, the morality of targeted wartime killings, when compared with other possible policies, seems obvious. Such killings are clearly superior to the Left's preferred non-violent means of trying to oust dictators: economic sanctions. Such embargoes almost always punish the innocent (civilians of the targeted country) and sometimes even strengthen the guilty (the dictators who are able to play the besieged victim). In Iraq, sanctions have—if anything—helped impoverish the civilian population, without budging Saddam a bit.

Targeted killing can also be morally superior to waging all-out war. One of the reasons the Geneva Convention protects prisoners of war (POWs) is that soldiers are held blameless for state policies that they were presumably merely following, not creating. So, it's odd to consider it unacceptable to kill Saddam, but acceptable to kill thousands of his soldiers who may want nothing more fervently than to surrender to the nearest American. Indeed, the idea of proportionality in the law of war suggests that the means able to achieve an objective with the least destruction and killing—e.g., specifically targeting Saddam—is always to be preferred.

Critics of targeted killings still raise several practical objections to the idea. One is that it would prompt retaliation against U.S. leaders. But Saddam Hussein has already tried to kill an ex-U.S. president, George Bush in

Kuwait City, even with EO12333 still in force. And Osama bin Laden launched a hijacked airplane perhaps against the White House or the U.S. Capitol. The behavior of our enemies obviously isn't going to be positively influenced by our nice legalisms. In any case, the American president is now, and always will be, surrounded by the most sophisticated and tightest security in the world, executive order or no.

Another objection is that targeted killings simply don't make for good foreign policy. They fail and backfire. Even if they succeed, the resulting new regime can be hard to predict and control. All of this is true, and if we want to influence the course of a post-Saddam Iraq, an invasion six months from now may be preferable to killing Saddam tomorrow. But this doesn't mean that targeted killing shouldn't be an option. And, in the case of Iraq, an incipient invasion (giving us a military presence to control events on the ground) coupled with the killing of Saddam (to end the fighting quickly) may be the ideal scenario.

In the end, critics of the idea of targeted killings fall back on the assertion that it is somehow incompatible with American values. This is just Frank Churchism, a moral equivalence that condemns us for trying to kill first the people who are bent on killing us. It finds it intolerable that we might engage in any difficult or severe action in the course of defeating our mortal enemies, and perversely revels in any mistake, folly, or transgression we might commit along the way. It is this sensibility that splashes every American error in Afghanistan [during the war against terrorism] across the front pages, with the revelatory subtext that—aha!—we aren't so right and just after all.

[The September 11 terrorist attacks on America have] helped diminish, but not vanquish, this way of thinking. The Clinton administration initially wanted to try Osama bin Laden, then attempted to kill him by arguing that he was, in effect, a piece of terrorist "infrastructure" to be "degraded." The Bush administration has taken a leap ahead in clarity by frankly stating that Osama bin Laden is a person, just an evil one who deserves to be sent to his eternal reward as quickly as possible. As a terrorist bandit, bin Laden enjoys the protection of no international conventions against assassination or anything else. The same should go for Saddam Hussein, and other leaders in the future against whom we wage war.

For practical purposes, the ban on assassinations has recently eroded. The U.S. has over the last 15 years slyly targeted Muammar Qaddafi, Saddam, Slobodan Milosevic, and now Islamic terrorist Mullah Omar. But we should stop operating under the constraints of the Qaddafi rule, which holds essentially that if an attack on a leader is so imprecise that it might kill his friends and family, it's okay. The cleanest solution would be to add a definition of assassination to the executive order, making it clear that it doesn't forbid targeting a regime's military elite. This might offend the sensibilities of rogue-state leaders the world over, but so what?

"Rogue state" isn't just an idle phrase. It signifies a government that is operating outside of all civilized bounds. The U.S. now seems to be willing, not just to recognize this fact rhetorically, but to act on it with a policy of regime-change—which makes it very odd that we would insist on maintaining the polite norms of long ago, when every sovereign was a sort of brother. Saddam Hussein is a far cry from William Pitt. It is time we stop pretending otherwise.

6

The Ban Against CIA Assassinations Should Not Be Amended

Jonathan Fanton and Kenneth Roth

Jonathan Fanton is chair of Human Rights Watch, an international human rights organization. Kenneth Roth is executive director of the same organization.

In times of national crisis, such as the September 11, 2001, terrorist attacks on America, politicians are tempted to adopt any policy that seems to address the emergency. However, rash actions such as lifting the 1976 ban on CIA assassinations often create more problems than they solve. Allowing targeted killings of foreign leaders would constitute a violation of human rights and compromise the democratic values that America represents. Although international laws allow nations at war to target enemy troops as well as their commanders, such laws would not permit the CIA to assassinate terrorists such as Osama bin Laden during America's war against terrorism.

Dear President George W. Bush,

In recent days, the Administration and Congress have been urged to consider proposed policy changes as part of the U.S. government's response to the horrendous attacks of September 11. Human Rights Watch has already joined many others in publicly condemning this crime against humanity—a crime that is antithetical to everything we stand for. We believe strongly that those responsible for this atrocity should be brought to justice.

However, as the United States plans its response, we write to caution against ill-considered changes to U.S. law and policy that would put at risk the basic rights that were so brazenly flouted. Leadership from you and other senior officials is essential to ensure that any measures adopted in light of this tragedy are publicly debated, thoughtfully considered, and comply fully with international human rights and humanitarian law. We

From "U.S. Policy on Assassinations, CIA: Human Rights Watch Letter to President George W. Bush," by Jonathan Fanton and Kenneth Roth, www.hrw.org, September 20, 2001. Copyright © 2001 by Human Rights Watch. Reprinted with permission.

are particularly concerned about proposals to end the ban on assassinations and to ease restrictions on the CIA's recruitment of abusive informants.

Assassinations

One proposal has been to lift the ban on U.S. participation in assassinations. As you are aware, President Gerald Ford imposed this ban by executive order in 1976 following revelations by the Church Committee of CIA involvement in planned or actual assassinations of, among others, Cuban President Fidel Castro, Congolese Prime Minister Patrice Lumumba, Chilean President Salvador Allende, Dominican President Rafael Trujillo, and Che Guevara. A policy of assassination poses a dangerous risk of backfiring—the United States as an open society is particularly vulnerable in this regard—and is obviously a blatant violation of the right to life.

In the wake of the September 11 attacks, it has been suggested that the prohibition on assassinations handicaps U.S. counter-terrorism efforts, particularly as the nation girds for possible armed conflict in Afghanistan or elsewhere. In fact, the constraints imposed are no more than those essential to the maintenance of the values proclaimed by U.S. military and law enforcement officers.

First, it is important to note that even after the September 11 attack, existing policy does not impose undue constraints on U.S. military or police personnel. If the United States were to be engaged in an armed conflict in Afghanistan or elsewhere, international humanitarian law does not prevent military forces from targeting opposing troops, including their commanders (assuming that in other respects forces comply with international humanitarian law, including rules designed to minimize risk to noncombatants). Similarly, in situations in which law enforcement officials might seek to make an arrest, international policing standards allow them to use lethal force if strictly necessary to defend themselves or others from an imminent threat of death or serious injury. However, in both situations, international humanitarian and human rights law, as well as U.S. military and police doctrine, flatly prohibit executing anyone in actual or effective custody or targeting anyone who is not a combatant. To flout this prohibition during armed conflict would be a war crime.

Assassination poses a dangerous risk of backfiring . . . and is obviously a blatant violation of the right to life.

Moreover, lifting the prohibition on assassinations would circumvent criminal justice standards worldwide. U.S. officials have asserted that the organization believed responsible for the September 11 attacks has operatives located in perhaps dozens of countries. Declaring a "war" on this organization should not justify ignoring these standards any more than does the rhetorical war that is also fought against drug traffickers or the mafia. In countries where law enforcement cooperation is possible, the United States should remain committed to a criminal justice approach—investigation, arrest, trial and punishment, with all the guarantees of a fair trial that are central to any system of respect for human rights. Reverting to a policy of assassination would suggest that governments may pick and choose when these guarantees apply—with lethal results—even in countries committed to the rule of law. Such a policy would undermine global commitment to the rule of law and the most basic human rights, and America's credibility in championing those values.

CIA recruitment

Central Intelligence Agency guidelines adopted in 1995 do not prohibit the Agency from recruiting sources or informants who are involved in human rights abuse. They simply require headquarters approval before field agents can proceed with such recruitment. The allegation that these guidelines somehow prevent the Agency from using people with unsavory backgrounds to gain information about terrorist groups is thus hard to fathom. The guidelines clearly had nothing to do with the intelligence failure preceding the September 11 attacks. As CIA spokesman Bill Harlow asserted, "The CIA has never turned down a field request to recruit an asset in a terrorist organization."

In any time of national crisis, there is a temptation to embrace any proposal that appears to "do something" about the real dangers people face.

The guidelines do, however, provide a check against activities by field agents that would imply support for horrific human rights abuses. They were adopted following revelations that the CIA had maintained a paid relationship with Guatemalan military officials who had been involved in the 1990 murder of American innkeeper Michael Devine and the 1992 murder of Efrain Bamaca, the husband of American citizen Jennifer Harbury. Other paid CIA informants who have been responsible for violent abuse while on the CIA payroll include Chilean Col. Manuel Contreras, who helped to organize the terrorist car-bombing in Washington that killed former Chilean Foreign Minister Orlando Letelier and his American aide, Ronni Moffit; and Emanuel "Toto" Constant, whose paramilitary group FRAPH committed widespread atrocities during the 1991–94 period of military rule in Haiti.

The original rationale for the restriction must not be forgotten as reform proposals are debated. When an individual involved in ongoing violent abuse is put on the CIA payroll, there is a substantial risk that he will read his relationship with the United States as tacitly condoning his pattern of conduct. That risk is obviously less if the informant is a member of an organization plotting attacks on the United States, since no one would reasonably believe that the United States quietly endorsed attacks on itself. But the risk is quite real in the case of officials in abusive governments that might be enlisted in efforts to combat terrorism. It is easy to imagine, for example, a torturer who had joined efforts to fight terrorism understanding his CIA payments as implied endorsement of his inhuman methods. Both the rules and practice of the CIA should continue to discourage relationships with abusive informants whenever it is possible that the informant will understand the relationship to suggest tacit approval of an abusive course of conduct.

The easy way out

In any time of national crisis, there is a temptation to embrace any proposal that appears to "do something" about the real dangers people face. The changes being proposed are attractive to many because they can be made easily and quickly, unlike the hard, time-consuming reforms that might truly enable America's intelligence and law enforcement agencies to collect useful intelligence on terrorism. But the easy way offers no way out of the crisis that the United States has faced since September 11. All it does is threaten the very values that came under attack that day. Those are the basic democratic values we should now be redoubling our efforts to defend.

7

The CIA Has Too Little Accountability in the War Against Terrorism

George C. Wilson

George C. Wilson writes for the National Journal.

President George W. Bush has given the CIA extraordinary license in America's war against terrorism, and the CIA seems to be interpreting that mandate as an invitation to engage in "anything goes" operations. What is worse, the CIA is not being held accountable for its actions. For example, during the offensive in Afghanistan, the CIA killed innocent civilians with missiles, but it is unlikely that the operatives involved will be brought to justice as would be the case if military personnel were involved in such an attack.

The CIA fires Hellfire missiles from its version of the unmanned Predator drone aircraft and supposedly blows up innocent civilians in Afghanistan. Who picked the target? Who pushed the button? Will there be an investigation and perhaps a court-martial, which might be the case with a military officer whose mistakes killed innocents? Will the results of any such proceeding be made public?

Extraordinary freedom

Do ordinary Americans know how much freedom President George W. Bush has given the CIA? Is the agency employing other high-tech weapons against suspected terrorists, including urban-warfare devices the U.S. military is banned from using, such as electronic beams designed to render a crowd of people unconscious but not kill them?

The CIA is reportedly running a number of small hit teams in Afghanistan as a part of America's war against terrorism. My e-mails from abroad assert that Army and Marine snipers are among those American warriors detailed to the CIA in Afghanistan. The agency is also said to em-

From "Rogue Elephant's Return," by George C. Wilson, *National Journal*, February 23, 2002.
Copyright © 2002 by National Journal, Inc. Reprinted with permission.

ploy foreign mercenaries who are not subject to U.S. law. Would American citizens ever find out about it if one of these CIA-funded teams went wild in the boonies and committed another My Lai, the infamous Army massacre of South Vietnamese civilians that occurred 34 years ago?

Do we know even at this late date about the effectiveness, if any, of the granddaddy of remote-control attacks—the U.S. cruise missile strikes President Bill Clinton ordered launched in 1998 against terrorist training camps in Afghanistan? George Tenet, then and now the director of the CIA, refused to address the question when asked.

The danger is that some CIA operatives will interpret Bush's "go do it" mandate as an "anything goes" license.

The answer to those and other troubling questions about the CIA's expanding warrior role is either no, or, at best, perhaps not. Bush and Defense Secretary Donald Rumsfeld have said repeatedly since [the September 11, 2001, terrorist attacks on America] that, for the country's own good, they will not tell us about some American anti-terrorist operations. This is understandable, up to a point. The danger is that some CIA operatives will interpret Bush's "go do it" mandate as an "anything goes" license.

"It's not a risk-free situation," said former CIA Director Stansfield Turner when asked about this possibility. In an interview with *National Journal*, he said his feelings were "very mixed" about the freewheeling direction the agency is now taking. However, the retired admiral who directed the CIA for President Jimmy Carter from 1977 to 1981 doubted that a My Lai–type massacre could be kept secret, because "the whole system is so porous."

Lack of accountability

As for public accountability for misdeeds, Turner agreed that the CIA is neither as structured nor as transparent in this regard as the American military. He noted, though, that the CIA director has the power to punish agency employees for wrongdoing in a disciplinary hearing that is similar to a U.S. Navy captain's mast, a proceeding from which the defendant has no appeal.

Intelligence officials past and present note that CIA Director Tenet has an unusually unrestricted presidential mandate in this war. It essentially amounts to: "You know what needs to be done; go do it," a former CIA executive said. Such a bright green light, the ex-agent continued, could inspire the agency to return to the risky operations of the 1970s that prompted then-Senator Frank Church, D-Idaho, to call the CIA a "rogue elephant."

"It's already kind of scary when you have the CIA flying Predators around," a senior military intelligence officer who has operated in some of the world's hottest and darkest corners told me. "Who controls that? Who controls the targets? What are their rules of engagement? We in the military have to go by them; police officers have to go by them. What happens if some CIA operator in the boonies gets mad at an American general and decides to take him out? The CIA is becoming too technology-centric. It's not doing enough 'humint' [human intelligence gathered by painstakingly planted spies in target countries and terrorist organizations abroad]. The whole thing is fraught with danger, CIA-military overlap, and confusion."

James Bamford, author of *Body of Secrets*, who has been studying America's intelligence agencies for more than two decades and is now a visiting professor at the Richard and Rhoda Goldman School of Public Policy at the University of California (Berkeley), said the CIA has seized upon the armed Predator to regain some of the power it lost to the Pentagon, especially in overhead surveillance by satellite and aircraft.

"It's trying to flex its muscles after being neutered," he said. "But it's dangerous when they start overlapping with the military, because of the agency's lack of accountability. It should concentrate on collecting intelligence."

Bamford added that in the 1970s, Congress set up committees to oversee the CIA to protect the American people from agency excesses. "But the oversight committees have become cheerleaders."

Given the fact that our commander in chief is a President who delights in such cowboy talk as "Wanted, dead or alive," I think J. Kenneth McDonald, chief historian of the CIA from 1981 to 1995, had it right when he told *National Journal*: "I don't see a rogue elephant. But I certainly see the potential for one because of the open-ended nature of the war against terrorism."

8

A "Street" Fight

Evan Thomas

Evan Thomas is assistant managing editor for Newsweek *magazine.*

Contrary to the allegations of its critics, the CIA has been playing an effective role in America's war against terrorism. With the help of resourceful and courageous CIA agents—who infiltrated Afghanistan shortly after the September 11, 2001, terrorist attacks on America—the United States was able to rout the Taliban. Islamic terrorist Osama bin Laden and his cohorts will be much more vulnerable to U.S. apprehension without the Taliban protecting them. Moreover, despite the CIA's failure to anticipate the September 11 attacks, the agency is making inroads against terrorism worldwide.

Parachuting supplies to CIA operatives working behind enemy lines is a tricky business, even in an age of Global Positioning Systems and spy-in-the-sky satellites. Supplies meant for the Alpha or Bravo team sometimes land on the Echo or Foxtrot team. Last fall [2001] one frustrated spook, hiding at a secret drop zone near Kandahar, Afghanistan, sent this coded message to his handlers: "waited three hours through all possible windows: only one airplane passed and kicked off one bundle: some bags of beans and rice . . . and two bags of horse feed rpt horse feed. we do not have any f---ing horses."

Other CIA paramilitary officers did have horses, however. And they rode them to victory, in an improbable, partly planned, partly improvised assault on the Taliban [Afghanistan's ruling party until it was ousted in America's War against terrorism in 2001] that combined high-tech and ancient modes of war. The CIA's success in Afghanistan—the agency's ability to get on the ground quickly, join up with Northern Alliance fighters and guide U.S. Special Forces teams to the enemy—came as a surprise and a relief to many intelligence experts, inside and outside the government. There had been a rising tide of grumbling and at times outright mockery aimed at an intelligence service whose successes and failures over the years have been shrouded in myth.

The critics have not gone away. In recent books and articles a small but outspoken chorus of former CIA case officers has portrayed the once

From "A 'Street' Fight," by Evan Thomas, *Newsweek*, April 29, 2002. Copyright © 2002 by *Newsweek*. Reprinted with permission.

proudly swashbuckling agency as a timid, politically correct bureaucracy, overly concerned with being held to account by the press and Capitol Hill. Senior CIA officials interviewed by *Newsweek* concede that the agency has gone through some dispiriting times, a period of scandals, drift and second-guessing that reached a low point by about 1995. The agency was spread thin, losing disgruntled old hands and—in hindsight—insufficiently aimed at the hard target of terrorism.

Doing better than predicted

It is focused now. Though the CIA won't reveal details, the agency played a critical role in the massive raid staged last month [March 2002] against Qaeda operatives hiding out in Pakistan, including Abu Zubaydah, Osama bin Laden's key deputy charged with running terror operations on the ground. (Zubaydah was shot in the groin trying to flee. "If he's singing," said a CIA official, "it will be in a higher pitch.") Since 9-11, the agency has been deluged with job applicants and showered with dollars by Congress, enabling the CIA to add more case officers (the CIA refuses to reveal the total, but the overall number is surprisingly small). Well before 9-11, these officials contend, the agency was rebuilding its "clandestine service," the spy handlers who gather HUMINT (human intelligence) and run covert actions. The men at the top of the CIA do not predict miracles: creating a cadre of experienced case officers who can recruit and run agents inside terrorist cells is a very slow and chancy process. "We're about halfway there," said a top official.

The CIA's success in Afghanistan . . . came as a surprise and a relief to many intelligence experts.

How is the CIA really doing in the war on terror? The answer is: better than the agency's more vocal critics suggest. The more difficult question remains whether "better" is good enough. The CIA likes to say that its successes remain secret, while its failures (like a recently busted spying operation in Russia) make the headlines. Nonetheless, it is possible to get at least a partial look inside the shadow war. *Newsweek* interviewed present and former agency officials and knowledgeable outsiders to put together a picture of the agency's progress. While some intelligence experts remain gloomy, most agree that the CIA is making gradual headway against a very difficult foe. One major terrorist attack, of course, could make even that carefully hedged assessment sound like so much wishful thinking.

The resourcefulness and courage of the CIA men who infiltrated Afghanistan shortly after 9-11 is beyond doubt. *Newsweek* interviewed a member of the first team that went in, a former Army Special Forces soldier who joined the CIA in the mid-'80s. Rick (not his real name) shipped out with his team—two CIA case officers who speak Farsi and Dari, two former Special Forces operators (a former Navy SEAL and Rick), a communications specialist, a medic and three air crew—on Sept. 19, eight days after the terror attacks. On earlier missions into northern Afghanistan, agency case officers had nearly died in local helicopters ("flying coffins," said Rick), including one that had been chased by a Taliban MiG fighter. So the agency bought a better chopper from the Russians and stenciled on a memorable tail number: 91101. After 9-11, the agency did not wait to obtain landing rights from surrounding countries as it moved its team into northern Afghanistan, and it ignored the military's careful requirement that any commando raid be backed up by an "extraction plan" and search-and-rescue teams. If the CIA group got into trouble it was on its own.

As even Pentagon officials will concede, the CIA can move more nimbly than the military in these situations. It is lucky that the agency has any paramilitary force—its "special activities" group had atrophied after the cold war, dwindling to a skeleton force by 1997. It is also fortunate that the agency had maintained contacts with the Northern Alliance [who were fighting the Taliban for control of Afghanistan] through several earlier, unsucessful attempts to track and target [Islamic terrorist] Osama bin Laden. Landing in the northwest corner of Afghanistan on Sept. 26, Rick and his NALT (Northern Alliance Liaison Team) found their local allies willing to fight the Taliban but woefully lacking in supplies. The first mission was to call in airdrops of "beans, bullets and cold-weather gear," said Rick. (Many of the Afghans were wearing sneakers and sandals.) For themselves, the agency men requested good leather saddles, to improve on the wooden ones provided by their hosts. The NALT team was followed by five more six-men teams, Alpha in the northwest, Bravo at Mazar-e Sharif, Charlie in the west, Echo and Foxtrot in the south. The agency teams secured HLZs—helicopter landing zones—for military Special Forces who arrived with their laser target designators to enable American air power to strike Taliban positions. (Rick named his HLZ after his daughter.) Relations between the military and the CIA—touchy in the past—were relatively smooth. Rick was an old friend of the commander of the Fifth Special Forces. "I'd just pick up the SAT phone and call him," he says.

How is the CIA really doing in the war on terror? The answer is: better than the agency's more vocal critics suggest.

The NALT leader, Joe (not his real name), a case officer who had been about to retire with 30 years' experience when 9-11 happened, radioed back to Washington that he was "confident" the Taliban would break under bombardment. CIA Director George Tenet brought this on-the-ground evaluation directly to President George W. Bush. By the beginning of November, with little visible progress on the battlefield, some of Bush's top advisers were starting to wonder: is it time to send in heavy reinforcements of U.S. troops? But the agency's man was proved right: by early December, the Taliban was in full rout.

Uncertain allies

The CIA did have to cope with uncertain allies. The local warlords were sometimes more interested in fighting each other than the Taliban. And the Northern Alliance was thoroughly penetrated by Taliban spies, who reported back on the CIA's presence and location. At one point, a Taliban counterattack threatened to overrun one CIA-Northern Alliance position. While the CIA forces opened fire with automatic weapons, their Afghan protectors hid behind a rock. "Get up! Get up and fight!" shouted a CIA man. Came the reply: "This is not our village. This is not our fight." The CIA man shouted back, "What the hell does it look like? *I'm* from this village?" The Afghans joined in the battle and the Taliban was repulsed. The every-man-for-himself ethos showed up again at Thanksgiving. The CIA tried to airdrop frozen turkeys to its men, but the Afghans got there first. The Northern Alliance dined on turkey with all the fixin's. The CIA men ate beans.

Getting inside a terrorist organization is extremely difficult.

Some of the airdrops were bundles of $20 bills. The CIA "bought more Taliban leaders than it killed," said one official. The price tag was anywhere from $50 to $100,000 (always paid in U.S. dollars, the preferred currency). "A package of a million dollars looks about like this," said Rick, spreading his arms about two feet wide. Headquarters cabled the operators on the ground to inquire what steps were being taken to safeguard the cash. "We're sleeping on top of it," cabled back the team leader.

In December, when Al Qaeda and Taliban remnants fled into the mountains near Tora Bora, CIA team leaders warned that the border into Pakistan was "totally porous," said Rick. Central Command would not commit U.S. ground forces, and Afghan and Pakistani efforts to close the door were sometimes halfhearted. At the CIA no one was surprised when bin Laden and most of the top Al Qaeda leadership got away. "We are in full pursuit, and we will find them," a senior CIA official told *Newsweek*.

The challenge of infiltrating terrorist networks

The fall of the Taliban brought little celebrating at CIA headquarters in Langley, Va. "We understood that here comes the hard part," said a top official. "Even if we do catch bin Laden, the leadership will be quickly replaced. It's just like a drug cartel." Because the 9-11 attacks caught the intelligence community by surprise, it was widely assumed that the CIA had failed to penetrate Al Qaeda. Agency officials were exasperated when congressmen demanded to know: how come John Walker Lindh, a California teenager, could join Al Qaeda, while the CIA was shut out? In fact, say CIA officials, the agency had "scores" of assets reporting on Al Qaeda before 9-11, though only a few sources were actual terrorists. "So what?" scoffs Robert Baer, a former case officer and one of the agency's harshest critics. "They've got somebody whose cousin has a friend who knows somebody. All these sources didn't warn them about 9-11."

Getting inside a terrorist organization is extremely difficult. The notion that an American can work his way in by putting on a burnoose, speaking Arabic and "hanging around the mosque" is "cowboy stuff," says one top spymaster. During the cold war, the best CIA assets were all "walk-ins," disillusioned Russian military or KGB officials who "self-recruited"—offered their services to the Americans, sometimes to show their disgust with the communist system, sometimes for cash, often for both. In the war on terror, the most useful turncoats still walk in. Before 9-11, the CIA received on average about 15 volunteers a month offering to spy on Al Qaeda. After 9-11, the rate increased to 15 a day. Almost all are worthless—nuts, visa-seekers, scam artists. And the occasional useful walk-in is generally a "scumbucket," says a top spymaster—a thief, a kidnapper, or worse.

CIA officers have always been willing to take risks and go into the "street" to meet would-be spies. But in the mid-'90s, there was a reluctance to recruit assets who could become problem cases. At Langley, the bureaucrats were fearful of being dragged before a congressional committee to justify how they could have hired a "human-rights abuser." Now the cautious approach is "gone," says one high-ranking agency official. "We've sent out every possible guidance: we're taking risks."

The CIA often works with foreign intelligence services to penetrate terrorist groups. The services of some Arab states do not labor under the same constraints as the CIA. "The Egyptians, they're kick-a—. They can do things we can't do," says one CIA official. The Egyptians, as well as the Jordanians and probably others in the Middle East, have been known to arrest whole families in their quest for information. But foreign security services have their own agendas and divided loyalties.

In the past presidents had often turned to the CIA when all else failed.

One case officer described his attempt to enlist the services of an intelligence officer working for an unnamed country, a "state sponsor" of terrorism. At first, he got some help from an unusual source. In a casual conversation with the wife of the CIA case officer, the wife of the foreign intelligence officer volunteered that her husband had close ties to a terrorist group. The CIA case officer met with the woman, who offered to help the CIA gain access to her husband's files. But it might be necessary, the woman suggested, for her husband to have "an accident." "We don't do that," the CIA man explained. The wife seemed disappointed. ("It was an arranged marriage. She detested him," explained the agency man.) The woman agreed to help the CIA, even to take a lie-detector test. She stipulated that there were only two things she would not do: *personally* kill her husband or take off her burqa. "It was clear," the CIA man said, "that of the two, killing her husband would be easier for her." In the end, despite the wife's help, the CIA man never did make an agent of the intelligence officer. Sometimes the culture gap is too wide.

An unsure role

Navigating such treacherous and unfamiliar territory requires exceptional experience, subtlety and skill. Bedeviled by declining budgets and a hostile press and Congress after the 1986 Iran-contra scandal, the CIA became scattered, sclerotic, unsure of its post-cold-war role. From the perspective of 9-11, it's obvious that the agency should have zeroed in on global terrorism. But the agency's various "customers," the federal agencies who count on its intelligence gathering, were also interested in economic spying, nuclear proliferation, the war on drugs and other priorities.

Morale has greatly improved under Tenet, who became director in 1997. Though initially suspect as an outsider—he had been staff director of the Senate intelligence committee—Tenet became popular for his plainspoken and boisterous manner. A basketball and Motown fan who has been known to sing golden oldies in his office, Tenet wisely bonded with Bush by personally delivering his intelligence briefing almost every morning. After 9-11, Tenet's White House connection amounted to job insurance.

In its rush to catch up with Al Qaeda, the agency may act too hastily. One former official notes that almost all the Africa analysts at headquarters were arbitrarily re-assigned to the Counter-Terrorism Center. This ex-spook fears that the agency will go overboard and forget the reforms and controls of the past 30 years. On Capitol Hill the CIA still has to endure a grilling for its role in the 9-11 disaster. "The fact is we had a catastrophic intelligence failure. The whole reason we have an intelligence community is to avoid catastrophic intelligence failures," says one CIA official. Agency officials say that the investigators will turn up some missed signals but no major blunders that could have been reasonably foreseen and avoided. That remains to be seen: congressional investigations have a way of taking on a life of their own. Investigators will look closely at the poor handoff of information between the CIA and the FBI. In the meantime the agency will be scrambling to avert the next nightmare.

In the past presidents had often turned to the CIA when all else failed. Covert action is very tempting when diplomacy doesn't work out or the cost of military action is too high. In real life the CIA often does get stuck with Mission: Impossible. It should be no surprise when the real-world result is less than a success. The difference this time is that the stakes are so high—as high, or higher, than during some of the longest hours of the cold war. With an enemy fanatically determined to use weapons of mass destruction to kill as many Americans as possible, failure is not an option.

9

Covert Action Is Sometimes Justified

Thomas H. Henriksen

Thomas H. Henriksen is associate director and senior fellow at the Hoover Institute on War, Revolution and Peace.

Covert action, such as espionage and assassination, is justified when diplomatic means fail and military intervention exacts too high a price. Unfortunately, in the aftermath of CIA intelligence failures during the Cold War, the United States has come to disapprove of covert action and now relies on air strikes to achieve policy goals. Air strikes seem to avoid the costs associated with all-out war, but they have largely failed to oust dictators and end atrocities, and have made America look immoral in the eyes of other nations. In contrast, covert action invisibly accomplishes America's policy goals without provoking foreign disapproval. Indeed, the United States has a long history of success using covert action, especially during the Cold War. Even though the Cold War is over, covert action is still a viable method of promoting democratic ideals and economic development abroad.

Lord Acton's famous maxim about the corruptive influence of power is just as true with regard to "absolute" military force as it is with regard to power in the domestic political realm. He might even have added that command of unmatched technological prowess can blind policymakers to lower-profile, lower-cost ways to achieve their nation's goals. Some security problems can be solved with a sledgehammer, or only with a sledgehammer. But far more common are those foreign policy challenges that can be solved—or prevented altogether—by measures short of violent conflict, even where routine diplomatic instruments prove ineffective. As the reigning superpower, the United States must not eschew forceful diplomacy or violence *in extremis* when its strategic interests are at stake. But Washington's current overreliance on aerial bombardment as the weapon of second (if not first) resort diminishes America's prestige, sullies its espousal of a liberal-democratic new world order, and endangers

Excerpted from "Covert Operations, Now More than Ever," by Thomas H. Henriksen, *Orbis*, Winter 2000. Copyright © 2000 by Foreign Policy Research Institute. Reprinted with permission.

its strategic relations with other major powers. Less confrontational options can achieve U.S. goals without the "harmful side effects" that include a strained Western alliance and strained relations with China and Russia, not to mention civilian deaths and material destruction. That "less confrontational" option is covert or indirect action abroad, and it offers today, no less than during the Cold War, an effective alternative to the unacceptable risks and costs of military operations.

Kosovo and Iraq

The Yugoslavian bombing campaign in the 1990s and the long series of air strikes against Iraq raise afresh the issue of how and why America should pursue its foreign policy agenda. Kosovo made clear, to some observers at least, that the United States should not wade into middle-sized conflicts in places with unpronounceable names and little strategic value, no matter what the extent of human suffering. Americans cannot, after all, make the lions lie down with the lambs, everywhere and for all time. Other critics concluded that Washington should have done more sooner in Kosovo, deploying ground troops and risking casualties in order to win a battle for international moral conduct. But the first opinion gives short shrift to the consequences that an unchecked slaughter in Europe could hold for that continent, while the second appears impractical because the stakes—even in President Bill Clinton's view—were not worth courting the political problems that could result from the shedding of American blood in a distant country for obscure goals.

The ambiguous rationale for involvement resulted in an air campaign and not a *war*, a characterization that the Clinton administration scrupulously avoided. But as it turned out, the relentless air strikes, often against civilian targets, sapped the moral high ground that Clinton coveted. They failed to halt Belgrade's atrocities in Kosovo, damaged relations with China and Russia over a nonstrategic issue, risked NATO's unity, and left [Serbian president] Slobodan Milosevic in power. One is left to wonder whether the necessity of "doing something" to address a genuine humanitarian and political crisis could have inspired an earlier, more effective, and less violent response lying between the extremes of disengagement and war.

Covert or indirect action . . . offers today . . . an effective alternative to the unacceptable risks and costs of military operations.

To be sure, a reliance on air power reflects our technologically oriented civilization. High-altitude bombing promises to override historical complexities. But it ignores the fact that intractable ethnic and political conflicts are often resistant to technological quick fixes. It is not enough just to make low-tech regimes in places like Serbia and Iraq "hunker down." It means ridding them of their predatory leaders. And that requires a dramatic paradigm shift back to covert action as the policy option of choice. Such operations have often leveraged the preponderance of U.S. power to secure outcomes favorable to American aims, and their effectiveness stemmed in part from the perception in a target country that the United States had thrown its weight behind one side in a crisis. Direct military intervention proved unnecessary. Indeed, one might even conclude that direct military intervention, far from being the way to ensure policy success, is a proof of policy failure.

Indirect methods rely less on cutting-edge technologies and employment of force, and more on American operatives' mastering local politics, understanding different cultures, and learning foreign languages. Above all, they call for political judgment and continuous, anticipatory attention to the world beyond American shores. Briefly, they seek to strengthen local opposition forces against an adversarial regime so as to bring about prophylactic changes in governments.

Despite NATO's ever-intensified bombings of Yugoslavia, Slobodan Milosevic not only pursued his "ethnic cleansing" policies [against ethnic Albanians] during the bombardment, but also clung to power after signing the Balkan military agreement. Other dictators such as Libya's Muammar Qaddafi and Iraq's Saddam Hussein have also endured American barrages without capitulating to U.S. demands. Perhaps it is time to look to other means in dealing with "rogues" and criminals who build weapons of mass destruction or destabilize their neighborhood.

Measures short of war

Needless to say, the U.S. government should always take the conventional diplomatic steps available in order to advance American interests and promote regional peace and the cause of democracy and human rights when they seem challenged. But traditional instruments of statecraft—sanctions, presidential appeals or threats, and American largesse (read *bribes*)—will not influence iron-fisted adversaries. The really tough nuts, such as Iraq, Iran, North Korea, Serbia, and Cuba, will not be cracked by sanctions or modify their policies because a miffed U.S. State Department has withdrawn its embassy staff. Economic embargoes are even more problematical, since they hurt innocent victims in the sanctioned states. Even the resort to international tribunals to try wrongdoers for murderous acts, for instance in Rwanda or the former Yugoslavia, does not suffice to forestall determined criminals. Ex post facto arrests come too late to stop cold-blooded criminality, and most indicted war criminals remain at large under unenforced arrest warrants. International law, while enjoying a renaissance since the post–World War II trials, is still too weak a reed to lean on where weapons of mass destruction or ethnic cleansing are concerned.

That is why the United States since World War II relied upon two indirect and nonmilitary remedies to undo actual or potential adversaries: robust public support for reformers in target countries, and muscular covert operations. Above-board approaches have entailed financial and technical assistance to bolster independent media, grassroots political movements, radio broadcasts beamed into a target country, and exchange programs for students, academics, journalists, and other professionals. The rationale was to pry open closed societies such as those of the Soviet bloc. After the fall of the Berlin Wall, U.S. overt assistance was instrumental in turning out former communist leaders through elections in

Bulgaria, Lithuania, Romania, and Slovakia. While these measures are not viewed as covert operations, they constituted a form of intervention in another state's affairs, at least from the perspective of the electoral losers. As such, they blur the line between subversive and reformist ventures. The National Endowment for Democracy, established in 1983, has promoted democracy in scores of countries and fills overtly some of the same functions that the Central Intelligence Agency undertook covertly in earlier decades. But its reformist strategies will simply invite the early death of democratic elements in a North Korea, Libya, Iraq, or Syria.

Ousting a ruthless regime, when it becomes necessary, requires moving along the operational spectrum from overt to covert methods.

Ousting a ruthless regime, when it becomes necessary, requires moving along the operational spectrum from overt to covert methods. Obviously, not all detestable regimes warrant subversion, and not all the likely alternative rulers are a clear improvement. President Dwight Eisenhower, an enthusiastic employer of secret interventions, backed away from coup plans against Egyptian leader Gamal Nasser when he realized that the political conditions in that country differed greatly from those in Iran, where the CIA had helped to remove Mohammad Mossadegh from power. When President George Bush, to take another example, realized that no attractive prospects existed to stage a coup against Panamanian strongman Manuel Noriega, he opted for a military invasion. But when a viable alternative to an odious regime does exist, then covert action combined with good political judgment and professional execution can yield magnificent results. They are also far cheaper in blood, treasure, and political capital, as a glimpse at the historical record reveals.

To be sure, the record does include failures, most infamously the setback that took place in Indonesia in 1958, when the Eisenhower administration backed an inept rebellion against a communist-leaning regime, and the botched Bay of Pigs invasion of Fidel Castro's Cuba by 1400 U.S.-trained and -equipped exiles. But those exceptions prove the rule inasmuch as they reflected bad judgment and poor execution. Far more abundant is the evidence of cheap and easy triumphs on behalf of American interests and values that date back to the very founding of the republic. For instance, George Washington secretly used congressionally approved funds not only for intelligence gathering, but also for bribes to secure the release of hostages taken by Algiers. To check the Spanish-backed Creek Indian nation, Washington's secretary of state, Thomas Jefferson, advocated the dispatch of agents to rally other tribes against the Creeks. As president, Jefferson authorized and funded the first U.S. covert action against a foreign leader for preying on American ships. He dispatched the American consul in Tunis at the head of four hundred armed insurgents to oust the pasha of Tripoli. Although the operation was not pressed to the point of the pasha's downfall, it made him respect the Stars and Stripes and protected U.S. shipping in the Mediterranean.

One of the most masterful applications of covert techniques took place when President Theodore Roosevelt sought control of the Isthmus of Panama to build a transoceanic canal linking the Atlantic and Pacific. But the Colombian parliament obstinately refused to ratify a treaty its government had negotiated that provided for cession of the Canal Zone and construction of the waterway. Roosevelt might have beat the drums for a military expedition, but instead he encouraged an indigenous Panamanian rebellion and overcame Colombian resistance. Three days after the insurrection, Washington recognized the new Republic of Panama. U.S. warships prevented Bogotá from landing troops to suppress the uprising, and the admiral commanding the local Colombian fleet was bribed to steam away. Shortly afterwards, Panama concluded a treaty with Washington leasing the Canal Zone.

During World War II, the Office of Strategic Services [the CIA's predecessor] conducted numerous operations against the Axis, from counterintelligence activity to airdrops of weapons and explosives for guerrilla bands operating behind enemy lines. Of course, war gives a wide latitude to covert actions against a belligerent state, but is a given action less moral when its purpose is to *prevent* a war rather than to win one? The question answered itself during the four decades of the Cold War.

Covert operations as a fact of life in the Cold War

The post–world war era ushered in a unique ideological, military, and diplomatic rivalry between the two surviving global powers. Except for the conflicts in Korea and Vietnam, much of the struggle between Moscow and Washington was conducted beneath the threshold of open combat lest they provoke a nuclear showdown. Covert "black" operations, then and now, are much less confrontational than direct military interventions, so the United States embarked on operations to support friends and overthrow leaders that appeared to further Soviet designs. In 1948 Washington funded the Christian Democrat parties in Italy and France to prevent the Communists from taking over those governments, and throughout Western Europe the CIA served as "a covert annex to the Marshall Plan." Elsewhere, it helped the Philippine leader Ramon Magsaysay to overcome the communist-backed Huk guerrillas, and intervened to repel communist insurgents in the Greek civil war. In 1953 the U.S. government also played a direct, but covert, role in overthrowing the left-wing Mossadegh regime in Iran, thus paving the way for the return of the shah's rule, at a cost of less than $1 million. A year later, Washington mounted a successful covert operation against the communist-aided Arbenz government in Guatemala. Some estimates hold that it cost the United States only $8 million to help displace Salvador Allende's socialist government in Chile in 1973. None of these American-aided ousters escaped criticism here or abroad as illustrations of American "imperialism"—but no one can deny their effectiveness and efficiency. Under the shah, Iran modernized and moved into the ranks of major players in Middle East politics, while Chile after Allende gradually became Latin America's beacon of economic growth, political stability, and (eventually) democratization. Neither Iran nor Chile is cause for U.S. embarrassment. Indeed, both did much better than a pre-coup prognosis would have predicted from their histories.

The United States also responded at the height of the Cold War to Castro's attempts to spread Marxism through guerrilla warfare in the Latin American countryside. In Guatemala, it first trained the government's armed forces in counterinsurgency techniques. Critics retorted that the protracted civil war claimed tens of thousands of lives and that government forces committed atrocities. That is so, but Castroite infiltration started the war in the first place, both sides committed atrocities—as might be expected in a society beset with gaping economic inequalities and violent ethnic politics—and in any case, the atrocities were hardly the product of American policy. The bottom line is that Guatemala is far better off today than it would be had the Marxist guerrillas prevailed.

Covert "black" operations . . . are much less confrontational than direct military interventions.

Elsewhere in Central America, Washington faced more Cuban-instigated subversion that could not be easily dealt with by U.S. aerial bombardments and ground invasions. But thanks to U.S. military assistance to the elected civilian government of El Salvador and to the Nicaraguan *contras,* Moscow was denied further inroads in this hemisphere. If a policy is judged on its success in advancing a country's return to peace, economic growth, institutional stability, and reintegration of former rebels into society and elected positions, then the Reagan administration's approach in El Salvador must be applauded. In Nicaragua, the Sandinista regime was first challenged by the *contra* guerrillas and then defeated in the 1990 presidential election, much to the embarrassment of the surprised Sandinista sympathizers in the United States.

Against great odds, the Reagan administration also did much to bolster the prospects of Solidarity, the Polish labor movement, in the early 1980s. Washington secretly funneled covert financial assistance, supplied communications equipment, trained communications operators, and shared intelligence with the officially besieged, but popular, labor movement. Solidarity's survival and witness played a significant role in the unraveling of the Soviet Union. Likewise, the Reagan administration sharply escalated Jimmy Carter's small-scale initiative of training and arming the anticommunist *mujahideen* in their insurgency against Soviet occupation of Afghanistan after 1979. When the United States finally added Stinger missiles to the rebels' arms inventory, the Soviets lost the ability to control events on the ground from the air, and the proud Red Army, the victors of Stalingrad, were humbled by mountain tribesmen. That humiliation in turn unhinged the Soviet ruling elite, paved the way for the collapse of the Communist Party, and sparked the dissolution of the Soviet empire in Central Asia. It proved to be one of the most masterful paramilitary operations since World War II.

The Bay of Pigs fiasco began a twenty-year-long reaction against covert operations. Ronald Reagan's successful support of the Afghan *mujahideen* reignited the debate. Critics argue that U.S. support of those rebels ultimately enabled the Muslim fundamentalist Taliban to occupy much of Afghanistan and play host to Osama bin Laden, the Saudi businessman turned terrorist. But such a monocausal explanation distorts history to serve political motives. For centuries, Afghanistan has been a badly fragmented country. The Soviets relied on local puppets to maintain control in a classic "divide and rule" scheme, which deepened societal divisions. Reagan's intervention did not cause the cleavages among Afghanistan's mountainous tribes. It helped them to unite temporarily against the Soviet occupation, just as they had resisted British penetration in the previous century.

The Bay of Pigs fiasco began a twenty-year-long reaction against covert operations.

Still, the "blow back" phenomenon is cited as evidence against covert enterprises: that is, to manipulate foreign countries is to invite retribution down the road. Perhaps that is so—no one can read the future—but no covert action could possibly compare with such direct actions as emergency airlifts to Israel, the Persian Gulf War, and the ongoing U.S. military presence in Saudi Arabia and the gulf when it comes to provoking anti-American sentiments in the Middle East. And when compared with the results of Soviet interventions or Marxist-inspired movements in such places as Afghanistan, Angola, Mozambique, Ethiopia, Cambodia, Peru, and Vietnam, the aftereffects of American covert enterprises look much more praiseworthy. Today, Chile, Guatemala, El Salvador, and Nicaragua, for example, have more promising prospects for progress than ex-Soviet proxies such as North Korea, Vietnam, Yemen, Somalia, or Cuba. . . .

Covert operations: a realistic alternative

Admittedly the record of achievement of indirect measures is not perfect. But then, clear-cut U.S. military victories since the Second World War have been much more scarce. Even the apparent victory in the Persian Gulf is marred by the enduring presence of Saddam Hussein. Korea, Iraq, Bosnia, and Kosovo were limited conflicts with limited results, and the war in Vietnam was an outright American defeat. A number of covert actions, on the other hand, have had decisive and favorable results, and certainly worked far better than the bombing of Saddam Hussein or Slobodan Milosevic, or the cruise missile launches against Sudan or Afghanistan. Covert actions can succeed in cases where direct intervention might exact great costs in American lives, funds, and damaged international relations, and can promote democratic ideals and economic development without putting American force and prestige on the line. Critics retort that the record of covert operations has included bloody tactics, right-wing death squads, and human rights violations. But their opponents were equally ruthless. It is just that we have romanticized any revolutionary guerrilla with a gun and a redistributive doctrine.

All war is hell. But is subversive warfare worse than the collateral damage done to hospitals, schools, and houses by aerial bombardments? America's new-found reliance on the "immaculate coercion" of bombing from three miles over Iraq or Yugoslavia to attain our policy objectives has led us not only to eschew the deployment of land forces, but also to downplay indirect anti-regime ventures. In the case of Iraq, the Clinton team initially dismissed every anti-Saddam group as ineffective or antagonistic, rather than working to coordinate the movements. Likewise, when consideration of assistance to the Kosovo Liberation Army (KLA) was publicly aired, opponents called attention to the divisions within the KLA and contended that helping it would set a precedent for other ethnic groups bent on separation. Critics did not want NATO to be the KLA's air force, and argued that the KLA were poor auxiliaries because some Albanians trafficked in narcotics for profit as well as for arms. This complaint about the moral rectitude of operatives is an old worry. It troubled George Washington, who bemoaned the need to work with "ambiguous characters" in intelligence gathering. But just as the Allies in World War II dropped weapons, radios, and other supplies to [Yugoslavia leader Marshal] Tito's communist partisans, NATO could not pick and choose what partisans existed on the ground. In fact, a lengthy Western tutelage of the KLA or guerrilla groups elsewhere holds out the prospect of professionalizing a movement, purging it of corrupt fighters, and influencing it along democratic lines. This has happened to the bulk of Latin American trainees, whom the United States instructed at length in democratic civil-military relations. Revolutionaries hunger for the legitimacy provided by a major patron. It is far easier to affect a nationalist movement while it is in the malleable stage than once it comes to power.

Is subversive warfare worse than the collateral damage done to hospitals, schools, and houses by aerial bombardments?

In the final analysis, politics always makes for strange bedfellows, and states must usually choose the lesser of evils. To refrain from supporting all but the most pristine Jeffersonian resistance force is to paralyze oneself.

Covert actions in the past did push the envelope of normal and legal international relations. But the ambiguous nature of the Cold War blurred the distinction in international law between declared hostility and genuine harmony. In other words, the previous era was conducive to covert enterprises. A nation-state's recourse to self-defense, however, has always been lawful, and certain rogue leaders do constitute a clear and present danger. The "end justifying the means" controversy confronts policymakers whenever they undertake covert, or even overt, actions against another state. We should hold indirect operations to the same criteria as overt uses of force. Do they advance American interests? Do they meet established principles of armed conflict? Are they proportional to the goal? In cases such as Iraq, where ordinary citizens suffer under a cruel tyrant and the regime threatens its neighbors with brutal invasion, arguments against subversion of Saddam Hussein appear overly legalistic.

Only other nations perform dirty tricks

Subversion offends American sensibilities of fair play, the rule of law, and orderly turnover of government to another party following a free election. We like to think that dirty tricks are the tactics of less scrupulous governments. The amoral French, perfidious British, or treacherous Russians somehow seem better suited to skullduggery than the "apple pie and mom" Americans. Others disdain, or even revel in, criticism of underhandedness in the pursuit of national interests. But Americans take it to heart, launch congressional investigations, and editorialize against underhanded methods that blot our escutcheon. The only result is that extended bombing, outsized destruction, and indiscriminate death are somehow offered as more moral and justifiable, especially if the United States is willing to foot the bill for reconstruction.

At first blush, U.S. sponsorship of indirect operations runs counter to the multilateralism espoused by U.N. exponents. Such American ventures in the past might have appeared unilateral and self-serving. But here again circumstances have shifted as a result of the acknowledged ineffectiveness of the United Nations during the Bosnia war of the early 1990s. More recently, the United Nations had to stand aside while NATO conducted the military campaign in Kosovo. The dispatch of Nigerian troops to conflict-ridden Sierra Leone and the Australian-led force in breakaway East Timor were further recognition by the United Nations that its former peacekeeping missions had given way to dangerous peace enforcement operations beyond the means of its blue helmets. Indirect assaults against the Saddam Husseins and Slobodan Milosevics of the world may well assume the mantle of virtuousness now attached to humanitarian interventions. In any event, when Washington's actions are perceived as advancing the greater and common good, as distinct from its own narrow interests, multilateralist condemnation may be muted by reality.

By ruling out covert actions and by relying too heavily on air assault, the United States handicaps itself in the emerging, complex world. Responses to every local case of murderous behavior should not rise to the level of direct American military intervention. Yet, as the reigning superpower, we feel a responsibility to address a spreading crisis before it engulfs a region. Prudence dictates an alternative to massive air strikes and lopsided, no-casualty victories that will in time erode our moral standing and raise up a host of adversaries worldwide. In an earlier age, Eisenhower recognized the dilemmas when he privately lamented "that some of our traditional ideas of international sportsmanship are scarcely applicable in the morass in which the world now founders."

From the U.S.-Soviet bipolarity we inherited a blurring between war and peace that has shaped our current era. The lessons and options from the past can be applied to small-scale cold wars that we are likely to face in the Serbias and Iraqs of the future. Indirect applications of power will relieve our military overextension, reduce our exposure to combat casualties, skirt unnecessary confrontation, and spare us from assuming burdens that are not easily shed. How much less costly, more humane, and more effective would well-planned and well-executed covert operations be than our present reliance on aerial siege warfare?

10

Covert Action Is Never Justified

Ramsey Clark

Ramsey Clark, attorney general during the Lyndon Johnson administration, is an international lawyer and human rights advocate.

Covert action by the United States damages democracy by violating the trust of its citizens. Unfortunately, American government has been involved in covert action since its inception. Examples of covert action include CIA assassinations of foreign and domestic leaders who threaten U.S. interests, and the slaughtering of innocent civilians during wartime. These secret actions also exploit and impoverish the people of targeted nations. Covert action will doubtless continue because it is supported by international organizations, the media, and corporate officials who benefit from it.

Nothing is more destructive of democracy or peace and freedom through the rule of law than secret criminal acts by government. The fact, or appearance, of covert action by government agents or their surrogates rots the core of love and respect that is the foundation of any free democratic society. Every true citizen of any nation wants to be able to love her country and still love justice. Corrupt covert actions make this impossible. They are the principal source of the possibility that a contemporary American poet would conceive of the lines penned by William Meridith more than three decades ago:

> *Language includes some noises which, first heard,*
> *Cleave us between belief and disbelief.*
> *The word America is such a word.*

Despite common knowledge that the U.S. government is engaged continually in dangerous covert actions, some that can alter the futures of whole societies, most people cling desperately to the faith that their government is different and better than others, that it would engage in criminal, or ignoble, acts only under the greatest provocation, or direct necessity, and then only for a greater good. They do not want informa-

From "The Corruption of Covert Actions," by Ramsey Clark, *CovertAction Quarterly*, Fall 1998.
Copyright © 1998 by *CovertAction Quarterly*. Reprinted with permission.

tion that suggests otherwise and question the patriotism of anyone who raises unwanted questions.

A tradition of covert action

Among thousands of known examples of wrongful covert actions by the U.S. government, several will suffice to show how difficult the task and rare it is that truth is learned in time. For 200 years, the U.S. has coveted and abused Cuba. Thomas Jefferson spoke of plucking the Cuban apple from the Spanish tree. The Ostend Manifesto of 1854, intending to provide room for the expansion of slavery, which was confined by the Great American desert and the new Free States, remained secret for 75 years, though it was signed by the U.S. Secretary of State, William Marcy of New York, for whom the State's highest mountain is named; our Minister to England, James Buchanan, who would be elected president within two years; and the U.S. ministers to Spain and France. The Manifesto first warned Spain that "the Union can never enjoy repose, nor possess reliable security, as long as Cuba is not embraced within its boundaries." The U.S. then offered Spain money for Cuba with the threat that if it refused, "then, by every law, human and divine, we shall be justified in wresting it from Spain. . . ." With the effort to force Spain to relinquish Cuba secret, a major chance for peaceful resolution of the irreconcilable conflict between the slave states and free states was lost. His role at Ostend earned southern support for Buchanan in the 1856 election and took the country down the wrong road. We will never know how many manifestos like that at Ostend have secretly threatened and coerced foreign concessions, or led to war.

Nothing is more destructive of democracy . . . than secret criminal acts by government.

In Vietnam 30 years ago, with all of Charlie Company, including dozens of robust young American soldiers who shot and killed helpless Vietnamese women and children and many other U.S. military personnel witnesses to, or aware of, the slaughter at My Lai, few would imagine the murderous event could be kept secret. Yet few would deny the U.S. intended to do so. The tragedy barely came to light through the courage and perseverance of several men. Ron Ridenhour broke the story after personal inquiry with letters to the Congress. The hero of My Lai, Hugh Thompson, who ended the massacre by placing himself between the U.S. troops and surviving Vietnamese and ordering his helicopter machine gunner to aim at the American soldiers and shoot if they tried to continue, was removed from Vietnam, separated from the service, and threatened with prosecution supported by Congressmen Mendel Rivers and Edward Hebert. Lt. William Calley alone was convicted, confined to base for a while, and still enjoys government support. Only by the sacrifice and heroism of an unusual handful did the story become known, and even then there has never been an acknowledgment of wrongdoing by the U.S. The medal begrudgingly given Thompson in 1998 was for non-combat service. And My Lai is viewed as an aberration, an ambiguous aberration.

When Salvadoran soldiers of the élite Atlacatl Battalion, which trained in the U.S., massacred Salvadoran villagers at El Mozote, shooting even infants lying on wooden floors at point blank range, the U.S. government was able to cover up any public disclosure, even though top reporters from the *New York Times* and the *Washington Post* and a TV team from CBS knew the story. It was a dozen years later before the massacre at El Mozote was confirmed, and years too late to affect U.S. plans for El Salvador, or the careers of those responsible for yet another U.S.-condoned, and -inspired, massacre.

Assassinations

Just to list a few of the alleged assassinations conducted or planned by U.S. [intelligence] agents exposes the crisis in confidence covert actions have created for our country. Salvador Allende, Patrice Lumumba, Ngo Dinh Diem, Benazir Bhutto, with many questioning whether President John F. Kennedy and Martin Luther King, Jr., should be included, and U.S. planning for the assassination of Cuban premier Fidel Castro part of our public record, while air and missile attacks directed at Muammar Qaddafi of Libya and Saddam Hussein of Iraq missed their targets. Still, a former presidential aide, George Stephanopoulos, the Huck Finn of recent White House staffers, calls for the assassination of Saddam Hussein in a full-page editorial in *Newsweek*, and there is no significant public or official reaction.

CIA Director Richard Helms pleaded guilty to perjury for false testimony he gave before the U.S. Senate on the CIA's role in the overthrow of President Allende. He was fined, but his two-year prison sentence was suspended. But the American public is unaware of it, and Chile has never been the same. U.S. support for the overthrow of Allende was the essential element in that tragedy. For years, Patrice Lumumba's son would ask me whenever we met, first in Beirut, or later in Geneva, if the U.S. killed his father. I finally gave him a copy of former CIA officer John Stockwell's *In Search of Enemies*, which tells the story. Justice William O. Douglas wrote in later years that the U.S. killed Diem, painfully adding, "And Jack was responsible." Bhutto was removed from power in Pakistan by force, after the usual party on the 4th at the U.S. Embassy in Islamabad, with U.S. approval, if not more, by General Zia al-Haq. Bhutto was falsely accused and brutalized for months during proceedings that corrupted the judiciary of Pakistan before being murdered, then hanged. That Bhutto had run for president of the student body at U.C. Berkeley and helped arrange the opportunity for [then-President Richard] Nixon to visit China did not help him when he defied the U.S.

Our covert government's past is modest prologue to its new powers of concealment, deception, and deadly secret violent actions.

So we should not be surprised that patriotic Americans wonder whether, or even charge that, the U.S. government assassinated President

John F. Kennedy and our greatest moral leader, Martin Luther King, Jr.

We have been told time and again of the "Deadly Deceits" of our government, occasionally by career CIA officers like Ralph McGehee, by FBI agents, crime lab scientists, and city detectives like Frank Serpico. Major studies on the lawless violence of COINTELPRO, the Life and Death of National Security Study Memorandum 200, the police murders of Black Panthers Fred Hampton and Mark Clark, are a part of the lore of our lawless government.

And still the People want to Believe.

New evils, new powers of concealment

Our covert government's past is modest prologue to its new powers of concealment, deception, and deadly secret violent actions. Too often the government is supported by a controlled, or willingly duped, mass media, by collaborating or infiltrated international governmental organizations, and by key officials in vast transnational corporations.

The new evil empires, terrorism, Islam, barely surviving socialist and would-be socialist states, economic competitors, uncooperative leaders of defenseless nations, and most of all the masses of impoverished people, overwhelmingly people of color, are the inspiration for new campaigns by the U.S. government to search and Tomahawk, to shoot first and ask questions later, to exploit, to demonize and destroy.

It is imperative that the American people care about and know what their government is doing in their name.

The CIA is rapidly expanding its manpower for covert operations against these newfound enemies. The National Security apparatus, with major new overseas involvement by the FBI, is creating an enormous new antiterrorism industry exceeding in growth rate all other government activities.

U.S. covert actions and coverups are carried out against our own citizens within the U.S. with impunity. Paul Brodeur, in his recent memoir, describes the murderous FBI assault on the Mt. Carmel Church near Waco, Texas, in 1993, which killed 76 people, including 50 women and children. Writing of the FBI's Hostage Rescue Team, he says:

> The tear gas, which had been supplied by the military, turned out to be highly inflammable and probably caused the tragic conflagration that incinerated most of the compound's inhabitants, including some twenty innocent children.
>
> Attorney General Janet Reno defended the decision to attack the compound on the grounds that children there were being abused—an allegation that subsequently proved to be false—and that the hostage-rescue team was exhausted after a thirty-one-day siege. Apparently, neither she nor anyone else thought to suggest that another hostage-rescue team be brought in to relieve it. Whitewash investigations conducted

> by the Justice Department concluded that although errors were made, there was no way to avoid an armed confrontation with the Branch Davidians, and the whole affair was swept under the rug. Subsequently, it came to light that for days before the final assault, FBI agents had undertaken to unnerve the cultists and keep them awake at night by illuminating the compound in the flare of floodlights, by sending helicopters to hover overhead, and by playing music at full volume on loudspeakers. Ironically, few people in the nation's liberal establishment questioned the Bureau's conduct in the Waco holocaust—no doubt out of desire to avoid embarrassing the already beleaguered young Bill Clinton administration—so the outrage was left to fester in the paranoid fantasies of government-hating, gun-loving paramilitarists and psychopaths, until it emerged as a cause celebré two years later in the wake of the bombing of the Alfred P. Murrah Federal Building in Oklahoma City [by Timothy McVeigh].

The U.S. is not nearly so concerned that its acts be kept secret from their intended victims as it is that the American people not know of them. The Cambodians knew they were being bombed. So did the Libyans. The long suffering Iraqis know every secret the U.S. government conceals from the American people and every lie it tells them. Except for surprise attacks, it is primarily from the American people that the U.S. government must keep the true nature and real purpose of so many of its domestic and foreign acts secret while it manufactures fear and falsehood to manipulate the American public. The reasons for and effects of government covert acts and cultivated fear, with the hatred it creates, must remain secret for the U.S. to be able to send missiles against unknown people, deprive whole nations of food and medicine, and arrest, detain, and deport legal residents from the U.S. on secret allegations, without creating domestic outrage.

As never before, it is imperative that the American people care about and know what their government is doing in their name. That we be demanding of government, skeptical, critical, even a little paranoid, because not to suspect the unthinkable has been made a dangerous naiveté by a government that does unthinkable things and believes it knows best. We must challenge controlling power in America that seeks to pacify the people by bread and circuses and relies on violence, deception, and secrecy to advance its grand plans for the concentration of wealth and power in the hands of the few.

For 20 years, Ellen Ray, Bill Schaap, Lou Wolf, and Philip Agee, with the help of very few others, have struggled against all odds to alert our people to the perils of covert action. They started their lonely, courageous, dangerous struggle in what many want to think was the aftermath of the worst of times, but now we can clearly see the worst is yet to be. The American people owe an enormous debt of gratitude to these valiant few.

The role of *CovertAction Quarterly* is more important than ever. Those who love America should support and defend its efforts, against the most powerful and secretive forces, to find the truth that can prevent our self-destruction and may yet set us free.

11

The CIA Helps Promote Peace

Robert M. Gates

Robert M. Gates, a career intelligence officer, served on the National Security Council staff under four presidents and was director of Central Intelligence under former president George Bush.

When the CIA helped negotiate the 1998 Israeli-Palestinian accord, many Americans grew concerned that the CIA was expanding its mission. However, the agency has always played a prominent role in international negotiations and in monitoring cease-fires and treaty compliance. Indeed, the CIA has a longstanding role in helping to promote peace worldwide. Although such public activities involve more direct risks for the CIA, the agency will no doubt succeed in minimizing such dangers.

Much ado is being made of the Central Intelligence Agency's prominent role in negotiating the 1998 Israeli-Palestinian accord and its prospective part in carrying out the agreement. Both critics and defenders of the C.I.A. have expressed concern that this is a significant departure from—and an expansion of—the agency's traditional activities and mission.

The C.I.A.'s role in international negotiations

I disagree. The C.I.A. has played a prominent, if discreet, role in international negotiations and in monitoring cease-fires and treaty compliance for decades. For example, after the 1973 Yom Kippur war between Israel and Egypt, the agency and, more broadly, American intelligence monitored troop withdrawals and compliance with the agreement, which was negotiated under American auspices.

Beginning in 1969, the C.I.A. assigned officers to American delegations negotiating arms control with the [former] Soviet Union. The officers actually helped draft provisions of treaties dealing with the monitoring of compliance and provided the negotiators, often on both sides, with data on Soviet forces. After Congress ratified these treaties, the C.I.A. was

From "The C.I.A.'s Little-Known Resume," by Robert M. Gates, *New York Times*, October 29, 1998. Copyright © 1998 by The New York Times Company. Reprinted with permission.

responsible for reporting suspected Soviet violations, and did so reliably.

In May 1990, President George Bush asked me, as deputy national security adviser, to go to India and Pakistan to see if we could reduce tensions that seemed to be building toward war. I took with me an offer to have the C.I.A. monitor the borders and share information with both sides to provide reassurance that no surprise attack was being prepared.

The C.I.A. [has a] longstanding behind-the-scenes role in helping to wage peace.

The agency's involvement in the Israeli-Palestinian agreement is more visible than in the past. But it is a realistic manifestation of the credibility the C.I.A. has built with both parties in its previous informal role in the region. Also, both sides plainly trust the agency more than they trust each other, and probably more than they trust other parts of the United States Government.

Attendant risks

There are risks in the C.I.A.'s involvement. The two sides, but especially Yasir Arafat and the Palestinians, run the risk of being labeled "C.I.A. stooges." Indeed, such accusations are already being hurled.

There is also a risk of "mission creep," where the C.I.A.'s role is gradually expanded. If the agency successfully performs its role in carrying out the accord, diplomats and political leaders may want to involve it in negotiations in other conflicts—an expanded mission for which it lacks resources and one that would inevitably cause turf problems with other parts of the Government.

There are more direct risks for the C.I.A. Its public involvement could become politically awkward if the agreement falters or the parties begin to quarrel over issues in which the agency plays the role of "honest broker" and gets caught between the sides. The C.I.A. could also come under pressure from the Israelis, Palestinians or even our own Government to hedge, soften or otherwise alter its assessments.

Finally, the new public role will increase the physical risk to officers in the field from extremists opposed to the agreements. None of these risks are new to the C.I.A., and based on experience, I am confident that the professionalism—and integrity—of C.I.A. officers will help reduce the dangers.

Although the publicity is a new (and doubtless unwelcome) experience, it seems fitting in this new era of openness that the C.I.A.'s longstanding behind-the-scenes role in helping to wage peace should finally become public alongside its long history in waging covert war.

12
The CIA Promotes Violence

Steve Kangas

Steve Kangas was a well-known champion of liberal causes and creator of the award-winning website Liberalism Resurgent. Kangas died in February 1999.

The CIA promotes political unrest, human rights violations, and military coups worldwide. The agency uses appalling tactics, including propaganda, purchased elections, blackmail, kidnapping, torture, death squads, and assassination. The CIA justifies these methods as necessary to fight the war against communism, but most of the CIA's actions are undertaken to protect America's economic interests abroad. More specifically, the agency protects the interests of wealthy Americans—who exploit the workers in developing nations such as Nicaragua and Iran—at the expense of poorer Americans who must pay the price for wars stemming from CIA actions. In light of these atrocities, the CIA should be abolished.

CIA operations follow the same recurring script. First, American business interests abroad are threatened by a popular or democratically elected leader. The people support their leader because he intends to conduct land reform, strengthen unions, redistribute wealth, nationalize foreign-owned industry, and regulate business to protect workers, consumers and the environment. So, on behalf of American business, and often with their help, the CIA mobilizes the opposition. First it identifies right-wing groups within the country (usually the military), and offers them a deal: "We'll put you in power if you maintain a favorable business climate for us." The Agency then hires, trains and works with them to overthrow the existing government (usually a democracy). It uses every trick in the book: propaganda, stuffed ballot boxes, purchased elections, extortion, blackmail, sexual intrigue, false stories about opponents in the local media, infiltration and disruption of opposing political parties, kidnapping, beating, torture, intimidation, economic sabotage, death squads and even assassination. These efforts culminate in a military coup, which

Excerpted from "A Timeline of CIA Atrocities," by Steve Kangas, Liberalism Resurgent, www.korpios.org, 1998. Copyright © 1998 by Steve Kangas. Reprinted with permission.

installs a right-wing dictator. The CIA trains the dictator's security apparatus to crack down on the traditional enemies of big business, using interrogation, torture and murder. The victims are said to be "communists," but almost always they are just peasants, liberals, moderates, labor union leaders, political opponents and advocates of free speech and democracy. Widespread human rights abuses follow.

"School of the Americas"

This scenario has been repeated so many times that the CIA actually teaches it in a special school, the notorious "School of the Americas." (It opened in Panama but later moved to Fort Benning, Georgia.) Critics have nicknamed it the "School of the Dictators" and "School of the Assassins." Here, the CIA trains Latin American military officers how to conduct coups, including the use of interrogation, torture and murder.

The Association for Responsible Dissent estimates that by 1987, 6 million people had died as a result of CIA covert operations. Former State Department official William Blum correctly calls this an "American Holocaust."

The CIA justifies these actions as part of its war against communism. But most *coups* do not involve a communist threat. Unlucky nations are targeted for a wide variety of reasons: not only threats to American business interests abroad, but also liberal or even moderate social reforms, political instability, the unwillingness of a leader to carry out Washington's dictates, and declarations of neutrality in the Cold War. Indeed, nothing has infuriated CIA Directors quite like a nation's desire to stay out of the Cold War.

The ironic thing about all this intervention is that it frequently fails to achieve American objectives. Often the newly installed dictator grows comfortable with the security apparatus the CIA has built for him. He becomes an expert at running a police state. And because the dictator knows he cannot be overthrown, he becomes independent and defiant of Washington's will. The CIA then finds it cannot overthrow him, because the police and military are under the dictator's control, afraid to cooperate with American spies for fear of torture and execution. The only two options for the U.S at this point are impotence or war. Examples of this "boomerang effect" include the Shah of Iran, General Manuel Noriega and Iraqi President Saddam Hussein. The boomerang effect also explains why the CIA has proven highly successful at overthrowing democracies, but a wretched failure at overthrowing dictatorships.

The following [examples] should confirm that the CIA as we know it should be abolished and replaced by a true information-gathering and analysis organization. The CIA cannot be reformed—it is institutionally and culturally corrupt. . . .

1953

Iran—CIA overthrows the democratically elected Mohammed Mossadegh in a military coup, after he threatened to nationalize British oil. The CIA replaces him with a dictator, the Shah of Iran, whose secret police, SAVAK, is as brutal as the Gestapo. . . .

1954

Guatemala—CIA overthrows the democratically elected Jacob Arbenz in a military coup. Arbenz has threatened to nationalize the Rockefeller-owned United Fruit Company, in which CIA Director Allen Dulles also owns stock. Arbenz is replaced with a series of right-wing dictators whose bloodthirsty policies will kill over 100,000 Guatemalans in the next 40 years. . . .

1959

Haiti—The U.S. military helps "Papa Doc" Duvalier become dictator of Haiti. He creates his own private police force, the "Tonton Macoutes," who terrorize the population with machetes. They will kill over 100,000 during the Duvalier family reign. The U.S. does not protest their dismal human rights record. . . .

1961

Dominican Republic—The CIA assassinates Rafael Trujillo, a murderous dictator Washington has supported since 1930. Trujillo's business interests have grown so large (about 60 percent of the economy) that they have begun competing with American business interests. . . .
Congo (Zaire)—The CIA assassinates the democratically elected Patrice Lumumba. However, public support for Lumumba's politics runs so high that the CIA cannot clearly install his opponents in power. Four years of political turmoil follow. . . .

1964

Brazil—A CIA-backed military coup overthrows the democratically elected government of Joao Goulart. The junta that replaces it will, in the next two decades, become one of the most bloodthirsty in history. General Castelo Branco will create Latin America's first death squads, or bands of secret police who hunt down "communists" for torture, interrogation and murder. Often these "communists" are no more than Branco's political opponents. Later it is revealed that the CIA trains the death squads. . . .

1969

Uruguay—The notorious CIA torturer Dan Mitrione arrives in Uruguay, a country torn with political strife. Whereas right-wing forces previously used torture only as a last resort, Mitrione convinces them to use it as a routine, widespread practice. "The precise pain, in the precise place, in the precise amount, for the desired effect," is his motto. The torture techniques he teaches to the death squads rival the Nazis'. He eventually becomes so feared that revolutionaries will kidnap and murder him a year later.

1970

Cambodia—The CIA overthrows Prince Sahounek, who is highly popular among Cambodians for keeping them out of the Vietnam War. He is replaced by CIA puppet Lon Nol, who immediately throws Cambodian troops into battle. This unpopular move strengthens once minor opposition parties like the Khmer Rouge, which achieves power in 1975 and massacres millions of its own people. . . .

1973

Chile—The CIA overthrows and assassinates Salvador Allende, Latin America's first democratically elected socialist leader. The problems begin when Allende nationalizes American-owned firms in Chile. ITT offers the CIA $1 million for a coup (reportedly refused). The CIA replaces Allende with General Augusto Pinochet, who will torture and murder thousands of his own countrymen in a crackdown on labor leaders and the political left. . . .

1975

Angola—Eager to demonstrate American military resolve after its defeat in Vietnam, Henry Kissinger launches a CIA-backed war in Angola. Contrary to Kissinger's assertions, Angola is a country of little strategic importance and not seriously threatened by communism. The CIA backs the brutal leader of UNITAS, Jonas Savimbi. This polarizes Angolan politics and drives his opponents into the arms of Cuba and the Soviet Union for survival. Congress will cut off funds in 1976, but the CIA is able to run the war off the books until 1984, when funding is legalized again. This entirely pointless war kills over 300,000 Angolans. . . .

1979

Iran—The CIA fails to predict the fall of the Shah of Iran, a longtime CIA puppet, and the rise of Muslim fundamentalists who are furious at the CIA's backing of SAVAK, the Shah's bloodthirsty secret police. In revenge, the Muslims take 52 Americans hostage in the U.S. embassy in Tehran.

Afghanistan—The Soviets invade Afghanistan. The CIA immediately begins supplying arms to any faction willing to fight the occupying Soviets. Such indiscriminate arming means that when the Soviets leave Afghanistan, civil war will erupt. Also, fanatical Muslim extremists now possess state-of-the-art weaponry. One of these is Sheik Abdel Rahman, who will become involved in the World Trade Center bombing in New York. . . .
Nicaragua—Anastasios Samoza II, the CIA-backed dictator, falls. The Marxist Sandinistas take over government, and they are initially popular because of their commitment to land and anti-poverty reform. Samoza had a murderous and hated personal army called the National Guard. Remnants of the Guard will become the Contras, who fight a CIA-backed guerilla war against the Sandinista government throughout the 1980s. . . .

1981

Iran/Contra Begins—The CIA begins selling arms to Iran at high prices, using the profits to arm the Contras fighting the Sandinista government in

Nicaragua. President Reagan vows that the Sandinistas will be "pressured" until "they say 'uncle.'" The CIA's *Freedom Fighter's Manual* disbursed to the Contras includes instruction on economic sabotage, propaganda, extortion, bribery, blackmail, interrogation, torture, murder and political assassination.

1983

Honduras—The CIA gives Honduran military officers the *Human Resource Exploitation Training Manual—1983*, which teaches how to torture people. Honduras' notorious "Battalion 316" then uses these techniques, with the CIA's full knowledge, on thousands of leftist dissidents. At least 184 are murdered.

1984

The Boland Amendment—The last of a series of Boland Amendments is passed. These amendments have reduced CIA aid to the Contras; the last one cuts it off completely. However, CIA Director William Casey is already prepared to "hand off" the operation to Colonel Oliver North, who illegally continues supplying the Contras through the CIA's informal, secret, and self-financing network. This includes "humanitarian aid" donated by Adolph Coors and William Simon, and military aid funded by Iranian arms sales. . . .

1986

Iran/Contra Scandal—Although the details have long been known, the Iran/Contra scandal finally captures the media's attention in 1986. Congress holds hearings, and several key figures (like Oliver North) lie under oath to protect the intelligence community. CIA Director William Casey dies of brain cancer before Congress can question him. All reforms enacted by Congress after the scandal are purely cosmetic. . . .

1991

The Gulf War—The U.S. liberates Kuwait from Iraq. But Iraq's dictator, Saddam Hussein, is another creature of the CIA. With U.S. encouragement, Hussein invaded Iran in 1980. During this costly eight-year war, the CIA built up Hussein's forces with sophisticated arms, intelligence, training and financial backing. This cemented Hussein's power at home, allowing him to crush the many internal rebellions that erupted from time to time, sometimes with poison gas. It also gave him all the military might he needed to conduct further adventurism—in Kuwait, for example. . . .

The dinosaurs should die

In a speech before the CIA celebrating its 50th anniversary, President Bill Clinton said: "By necessity, the American people will never know the full story of your courage."

Clinton's is a common defense of the CIA: namely, the American people should stop criticizing the CIA because they don't know what it *really* does. This, of course, is the heart of the problem in the first place. An agency that is above criticism is also above moral behavior and reform. Its secrecy and lack of accountability allows its corruption to grow unchecked.

Furthermore, Clinton's statement is simply untrue. The history of the agency is growing painfully clear, especially with the declassification of historical CIA documents. We may not know the details of *specific* operations, but we do know, quite well, the *general* behavior of the CIA. These facts began emerging nearly two decades ago at an ever-quickening pace. Today we have a remarkably accurate and consistent picture, repeated in country after country, and verified from countless different directions.

The CIA's response to this growing knowledge and criticism follows a typical historical pattern. (Indeed, there are remarkable parallels to the Medieval Church's fight against the Scientific Revolution.) The first journalists and writers to reveal the CIA's criminal behavior were harassed and censored if they were American writers, and tortured and murdered if they were foreigners. However, over the last two decades the tide of evidence has become overwhelming, and the CIA has found that it does not have enough fingers to plug every hole in the dike. This is especially true in the age of the Internet, where information flows freely among millions of people. Since censorship is impossible, the Agency must now defend itself with apologetics. Clinton's "Americans will never know" defense is a prime example.

Another common apologetic is that "the world is filled with unsavory characters, and we must deal with them if we are to protect American interests at all." There are two things wrong with this. First, it ignores the fact that the CIA has regularly spurned alliances with defenders of democracy, free speech and human rights, preferring the company of military dictators and tyrants. The CIA had moral options available to them, but did not take them.

Second, this argument begs several questions. The first is: "*Which* American interests?" The CIA has courted right-wing dictators because they allow *wealthy* Americans to exploit the country's cheap labor and resources. But poor and middle-class Americans pay the price whenever they fight the wars that stem from CIA actions, from Vietnam to the Gulf War to Panama. The second begged question is: "Why should American interests come at the expense of other peoples' human rights?"

The CIA should be abolished, its leadership dismissed and its relevant members tried for crimes against humanity. Our intelligence community should be rebuilt from the ground up, with the goal of collecting and analyzing information. As for covert action, there are two moral options. The first one is to eliminate covert action completely. But this gives jitters to people worried about the Adolf Hitlers of the world. So a second option is that we can place covert action under extensive and true democratic oversight. For example, a bipartisan Congressional Committee of 40 members could review and veto all aspects of CIA operations upon a majority or super-majority vote. Which of these two options is best may be the subject of debate, but one thing is clear: like dictatorship, like monarchy, unaccountable covert operations should die like the dinosaurs they are.

13

The CIA Has Been Involved in Drug Trafficking

Gary Webb

Gary Webb has been an investigative reporter for over twenty years, focusing on government and private sector corruption and winning more than thirty journalism awards. Webb is currently a consultant to the California State Legislature's Task Force on Government Oversight. Webb is also author of the book Dark Alliance: The CIA, the Contras, and the Crack Cocaine Explosion, *from which this excerpt was taken.* Dark Alliance *originally appeared as a controversial series published in 1996 in the* San Jose Mercury News.

Money derived from drug trafficking in the United States during the 1980s was being used to fund the Nicaraguan Contras, who were trying to overthrow the ruling Sandinista regime. In 1992, a drug smuggler with connections to the Contras named Danilo Blandón was indicted for drug trafficking and was ordered held in jail without bail because he posed a serious threat. Oddly, however, Blandón and his associates all received unusually light sentences, which looked suspicious given the fact that the case against them was supposedly airtight. Further investigation into the matter revealed that a U.S. attorney secretly had Blandón's sentences cut twice by telling the judge that he had cooperated with and assisted the United States as an informant. These discoveries led to the supposition that the U.S. government was protecting several known drug traffickers whose drug deals were funding the CIA-backed Contras in Nicaragua. In addition, Contra leaders acknowledged receiving profits from drug trafficking in Los Angeles, with the apparent knowledge of the CIA. Other reporters investigating the connection between the CIA, the Contras, and cocaine trafficking were discouraged from pursuing their investigations by the newspapers they worked for and were harassed by congressional representatives.

Editor's note: Gary Webb's Dark Alliance series prompted an internal investigation by the CIA, whose 1998 report denies the agency's complicity in drug traf-

Excerpted from *Dark Alliance: The CIA, the Contras, and the Crack Cocaine Explosion*, by Gary Webb (New York: Seven Stories Press, 1998). Copyright © 1998 by Gary Webb. Reprinted by permission of the publisher.

ficking to fund the Nicaraguan Contras. Most major newspapers backed away from Webb's allegations, and he quit the San Jose Mercury News *in 1997 due to conflicts that developed over his investigations.*

When I came to work in the sprawling newsroom of the *Cleveland Plain Dealer* in the early 1980s, I was assigned to share a computer terminal with a tall middle-aged reporter with a long, virtually unpronounceable Polish name. To save time, people called him Tom A.

To me, arriving from a small daily in Kentucky, Tom A. was the epitome of the hard-boiled big-city newspaperman. The city officials he wrote about and the editors who mangled his copy were "fuckinjerks." A question prompting an affirmative response would elicit "fuckin-a-tweetie" instead of "yes." And when his phone rang he would say, "It's the Big One," before picking up the receiver.

"One of the government's witnesses is a guy who used to work with the CIA selling drugs."

No matter how many times I heard that, I always laughed. The Big One was the reporter's holy grail—the tip that led you from the daily morass of press conferences and cop calls on to the trail of The Biggest Story You'd Ever Write, the one that would turn the rest of your career into an anticlimax. I never knew if it was cynicism or optimism that made him say it, but deep inside, I thought he was jinxing himself.

The Big One, I believed, would be like a bullet with your name on it. You'd never hear it coming. And almost a decade later, long after Tom A., the *Plain Dealer*, and I had parted company, that's precisely how it happened. I didn't even take the call.

It manifested itself as a pink While You Were Out message slip left on my desk in July 1995.

The big one

There was no message, just a woman's name and a phone number, somewhere in the East Bay.

I called, but there was no answer, so I put the message aside. If I have time, I told myself, I'll try again later.

Several days later an identical message slip appeared. Its twin was still sitting on a pile of papers at the edge of my desk.

This time the woman was home.

"I saw the story you did a couple weeks ago," she began. "The one about the drug seizure laws. I thought you did a good job."

"Thanks a lot," I said, and I meant it. She was the first reader who'd called about that story, a front-page piece in the *San Jose Mercury News* about a convicted cocaine trafficker who, without any formal legal training, had beaten the U.S. Justice Department in court three straight times and was on the verge of flushing the government's multibillion-dollar asset forfeiture program right down the toilet. The inmate, a lifer, had argued that losing your property *and* going to jail was like being punished twice for the same crime—double jeopardy—and seventeen judges from the Ninth Circuit Court of Appeals agreed with him. (Faced with the prospect of setting thousands of dopers free or returning billions in seized property, the U.S. Supreme Court would later overturn two of its own rulings in order to kill off the inmate's suit.)

"You didn't just give the government's side of it," she continued. "The other stories I read about the case were like, 'Omigod, they're going to let drug dealers out of jail. Isn't this terrible?'"

I asked what I could do for her.

"My boyfriend is in a situation like that," she said, "and I thought it might make a good follow-up story for you. What the government has done to him is unbelievable."

"Your boyfriend?"

"He's in prison right now on cocaine trafficking charges. He's been in jail for three years."

"How much more time has he got?"

"Well, that's just it," she said. "He's never been brought to trial. He's done three years already, and he's never been convicted of anything."

"He must have waived his speedy trial rights," I said.

"No, none of them have," she said. "There are about five or six guys who were indicted with him, and most of them are still waiting to be tried, too. They want to go to trial because they think it's a bullshit case. Rafael keeps writing letters to the judge and the prosecutor, saying, you know, try me or let me go."

"Rafael's your boyfriend?"

"Yes. Rafael Corñejo."

"He's Colombian?"

"No, Nicaraguan. But he's lived in the Bay Area since he was like two or something."

It's interesting, I thought, but not the kind of story likely to excite my editors. Some drug dealers don't like being in jail? Oh.

"What's the connection to the forfeiture story?" I asked.

Rafael, she explained, had been a very successful "businessman," and the government, under the asset forfeiture program, had seized and sold his automobiles, his houses, and his businesses, emptied his bank accounts, and left him without enough money to hire a lawyer. He had a court-appointed lawyer, she said, who was getting paid by the hour and didn't seem to care how long the case took.

"I've copied every single piece of paper that's been filed in Rafael's case and I can document everything I'm telling you."

"Rafael had the most gorgeous house out in Lafayette, and the government sold it for next to nothing. Now what happens if he's acquitted? He spends three or four years in jail for a crime he didn't commit, and when he gets out, someone else is living in his house. I mean, what kind of a country is this? I think it would make a good story."

It might, I told her, if I hadn't done it half a dozen times already. Two years earlier, I'd written a series for the *Mercury* called "The Forfeiture Racket," about the police in California busting into private homes and taking furniture, televisions, Nintendo games, belt buckles, welfare checks, snow tires, and loose change under the guise of cracking down on drug traffickers. Many times they'd never file charges, or the charges would be dropped once the victims signed over the loot.

The series created such an outcry that the California legislature had abolished the forfeiture program a few weeks later. But I knew what I would hear if I pitched the woman's story to my editors: We've done that already. And that was what I told her.

She was not dissuaded.

"There's something about Rafael's case that I don't think you would have ever done before," she persisted. "One of the government's witnesses is a guy who used to work with the CIA selling drugs. Tons of it."

"What now?" I wasn't sure I'd heard correctly.

"The CIA. He used to work for them or something. He's a Nicaraguan too. Rafael knows him, he can tell you. He told me the guy had admitted bringing four tons of cocaine into the country. Four tons! And if that's what he's admitted to, you can imagine how much it really was. And now he's back working for the government again."

I put down my pen. She'd sounded so rational. Where did this CIA stuff come from? In seventeen years of investigative reporting, I had ended up doubting the credibility of every person who ever called me with a tip about the CIA.

The escape charges were in fact the product of an unsubstantiated accusation by a fellow inmate, a convicted swindler. They were later thrown out of court.

I flashed on Eddie Johnson, a conspiracy theorist who would come bopping into the *Kentucky Post*'s newsroom every so often with amazing tales of intrigue and corruption. Interviewing Eddie was one of the rites of passage at the *Post*. Someone would invariably send him over to the newest reporter on the staff to see how long it took the rookie to figure out he was spinning his wheels.

Suddenly I remembered who I was talking to—a cocaine dealer's moll.

That explained it.

"Oh, the CIA. Well, you're right. I've never done any stories about the CIA. I don't run across them too often here in Sacramento. See, I mostly cover *state* government—"

"You probably think I'm crazy, right?"

"No, no," I assured her. "You know, could be true, who's to say? When it comes to the CIA, stranger things have happened."

There was a short silence, and I could hear her exhale sharply.

"How dare you treat me like I'm an idiot," she said evenly. "You don't even know me. I work for a law firm. I've copied every single piece of paper that's been filed in Rafael's case and I can document everything I'm telling you. You can ask Rafael, and he can tell you himself. What's so hard about coming over and at least taking a look at this stuff?"

"That's a fair question," I allowed. Now, what was my answer? Because I lied and I do think you're crazy? Or because I'm too lazy to get up and chase a story that appears to have a one-in-a-thousand chance of being true?

The Contras had been a creation of the CIA, the darlings of the Reagan Right.

"You say you can document this?"

"Absolutely. I have all the files here at home. You're welcome to look at all of it if you want. And Rafael can tell you—" In the background a child began yowling. "Just a minute, will you? That's my daughter. She just fell down."

The phone thunked on the other end, and I heard footsteps retreating into the distance.

Well, that's a promising sign, I thought. Were she a raving dope fiend, they wouldn't let her raise an infant. She came back on, bouncing the sobbing toddler. I asked her where she lived.

"Oakland. But Rafael's got a court date in San Francisco coming up in a couple weeks. Why don't I meet you at the courthouse? That way you can sit in on the hearing, and if you're interested we could get lunch or something and talk."

That cinched it. Now the worst that could happen was lunch in San Francisco in mid-July, away from the phones and the editors. And, who knows, there was an off chance she was telling the truth.

"Okay, fine," I said. "But bring some of those records with you, okay? I can look through them while I'm sitting there in court."

She laughed. "You don't trust me, do you? You probably get a lot of calls like this."

"Not many like this," I said.

Checking the facts

Flipping on my computer, I logged into the Dialog database, which contains full-text electronic versions of millions of newspaper and magazine stories, property records, legal filings, you name it. If you've ever been written about or done something significant in court, chances are Dialog will find you.

Okay. Let's see if Rafael Corñejo even exists.

A message flashed on the screen: "Your search has retrieved 11 documents. Display?" So far so good.

I called up the most recent one, a newspaper story that had appeared a year before in the *San Francisco Chronicle*. My eyes widened.

"4 Indicted in Prison Breakout Plot—Pleasanton Inmates Planned to Leave in Copter, Prosecutors Say."

I quickly scanned the story. Son of a bitch.

> Four inmates were indicted yesterday in connection with a bold plan to escape from the federal lockup in Pleasanton using plastic explosives and a helicopter that would have taken them to a cargo ship at sea. The group also considered killing a guard if their keepers tried to thwart the escape, prosecutors contend.
>
> Rafael Corñejo, 39, of Lafayette, an alleged cocaine kingpin with reputed ties to Nicaraguan drug traffickers and Panamanian money launderers, was among those indicted for conspiracy to escape.

The story called Corñejo "a longtime drug dealer who was convicted in 1977 of cocaine trafficking in Panama. He also has served time in a U.S. prison for tax evasion. He owns several homes and commercial properties in the Bay Area."

"It could be a pretty good story. The Contras were selling coke in L.A.?"

This sure sounds like the same guy, I thought. I scrolled down to the next hit, a *San Francisco Examiner* story.

> The four men were charged with planning to use C-4 plastic explosives to blow out a prison window and with making a 9-inch "shank" that could be used to cut a guard's "guts out" if he tried to block their run to the prison yard. Once in the yard, they allegedly would be picked up by a helicopter and flown to a Panamanian cargo ship in the Pacific, federal officials said.

The remaining stories described Corñejo's arrest and indictment in 1992, the result of an eighteen-month FBI investigation. Suspected drug kingpin. Head of a large cocaine distribution ring on the West Coast. Allegedly involved in a major cocaine pipeline that ran from Cali, Colombia, to several West Coast cities. Importing millions of dollars worth of cocaine via San Diego and Los Angeles to the Bay Area.

That's some boyfriend she's got there, I mused. The newspaper stories make him sound like Al Capone. And he wants to sit down and have a chat? That'll be the day.

Meeting the tipster

When I pushed open the doors to the vast courtroom in the San Francisco federal courthouse a few weeks later, I found a scene from *Miami Vice.*

To my left, a dark-suited army of federal agents and prosecutors huddled around a long, polished wooden table, looking grim and talking in low voices. On the right, an array of long-haired, expensively attired defense attorneys were whispering to a group of long-haired, angry-looking Hispanics—their clients. The judge had not yet arrived.

I had no idea what my tipster looked like, so I scanned the faces in the courtroom, trying to pick out a woman who could be a drug kingpin's girlfriend. She found me first.

"You must be Gary," said a voice behind me.

I turned, and for an instant all I saw was cleavage and jewelry. She looked to be in her mid-twenties. Dark hair. Bright red lipstick. Long legs. Short skirt. Dressed to accentuate her positive attributes. I could barely speak.

"You're . . .?"

She tossed her hair and smiled. "Pleased to meet you." She stuck out a hand with a giant diamond on it, and I shook it weakly.

We sat down in the row of seats behind the prosecutors' table, and I glanced at her again. That boyfriend of hers must be going nuts.

"How did you know it was me?" I asked.

"I was looking for someone who looked like a reporter. I saw you with a notebook in your back pocket and figured—"

"That obvious, is it?" I pulled out the notepad and got out a pen. "Why don't you fill me in on who's who here?"

She pointed out Rafael, a short handsome Latino with a strong jaw and long, wavy hair parted in the middle. He swiveled in his chair, looked right at us, and seemed perturbed. His girlfriend waved, and he whirled back around without acknowledging her.

"He doesn't look very happy," I observed.

"He doesn't like seeing me with other men."

"Uh, why was he trying to break out of jail?" I asked.

"He wasn't. He was getting ready to make bail, and they didn't want to let him out, so they trumped up these phony escape charges. Now, because he's under indictment for escape, he isn't eligible for bail anymore."

Blandón was involved with the Contras and had been selling large amounts of cocaine in Los Angeles.

The escape charges were in fact the product of an unsubstantiated accusation by a fellow inmate, a convicted swindler. They were later thrown out of court on grounds of prosecutorial misconduct, and Corñejo's prosecutor, Assistant U.S. Attorney David Hall, was referred to the Justice Department for investigation by federal judge Saundra Brown Armstrong.

(In a *San Francisco Daily Recorder* story about the misconduct charge, it was noted that "it is not the first time that Hall has been under such scrutiny. While serving with the Department of Justice in Texas, the Office of Professional Responsibility reviewed Hall after an informant accused Hall of approving drug smuggling into the U.S. . . . Hall said the office found no merit in the charge.")

She pointed out Hall, a large blond man with broad features.

"Who are the rest of those people?" I asked.

"The two men standing over there are the FBI agents on the case. The woman is Hall's boss, Teresa Canepa. She's the bitch who's got it in for Rafael."

As she was pointing everyone out, the FBI agents whispered to each other and then tapped Hall on the shoulder. All three turned and looked at me.

"What's with them?"

"They probably think you're my hit man." She smiled, and the agents frowned back. "Oh, they just hate me. I called the cops on them once, you know."

I looked at her. "You called the cops on the FBI."

"Well, they were lurking around outside my house after dark. They could have been rapists or something. How was I supposed to know?"

I glanced back over at the federal table and saw that the entire group had now turned to stare. I was certainly making a lot of friends.

Contra leaders . . . acknowledged receiving drug profits, with the apparent knowledge of the CIA.

"Can we go out in the hall and talk for a minute?" I asked her.

We sat on a bench just outside the door. I told her I needed to get case numbers so I could ask for the court files. And, by the way, did she bring those documents she'd mentioned?

She reached into her briefcase and brought out a stack an inch thick. "I've got three bankers' boxes full back at home, and you're welcome to see all of it, but this is the stuff I was telling you about concerning the witness."

I flipped through the documents. Most of them were federal law enforcement reports, DEA-6s and FBI 302s, every page bearing big black letters that said, "MAY NOT BE REPRODUCED—PROPERTY OF U.S. GOVERNMENT." At the bottom of the stack was a transcript of some sort. I pulled it out.

"Grand Jury for the Northern District of California, Grand Jury Number 93-5 Grand Jury Inv. No. 9301035. Reporter's Transcript of Proceedings. Testimony of Oscar Danilo Blandón. February 3, 1994."

I whistled. "Federal grand jury transcripts? I'm impressed. Where'd you get these?"

"The government turned them over under discovery. Dave Hall did. I heard he really got reamed out by the DEA when they found out about all the stuff he gave us."

I looked through the transcript and saw parts that had been blacked out.

"Who did this?"

"That's how we got it. Rafael's lawyer is asking for a clean copy. As you'll see, they also cut out a bunch of stuff on the DEA-6s. There's a hearing on his motion coming up."

I skimmed the thirty-nine-page transcript. Whatever else this Blandón fellow may have been, he was pretty much the way Corñejo's girlfriend had described him. A big-time trafficker who'd dealt dope for many years; started out dealing for the Contras, a right-wing Nicaraguan guerrilla army, in Los Angeles. He'd used drug money to buy trucks and supplies. At some point after Ronald Reagan got into power, the CIA had decided his services as a fund-raiser were no longer required, and he stayed in the drug business for himself.

What made the story so compelling was that he was appearing before the grand jury as a U.S. government witness. He wasn't under investigation. He wasn't trying to beat a rap. He was there as a witness for the prosecution, which meant that the U.S. Justice Department was vouching for him.

But who was the grand jury investigating? Every time the testimony led in that direction, words—mostly names—were blacked out.

"Who is this family they keep asking him about?"

"Rafael says it's Meneses. Norwin Meneses and his nephews. Have you heard of them?"

"Nope."

"Norwin is one of the biggest traffickers on the West Coast. When Rafael got arrested, that's who the FBI and the IRS wanted to talk to him about. Rafael has known [Norwin and his nephews] for years. Since the Seventies, I think. The government is apparently using Blandón to get to Meneses."

Inside, I heard the bailiff calling the court to order, and we returned to the courtroom. During the hearing, I kept trying to recall where I had heard about this Contra-cocaine business before. Had I read it in a book? Seen it on television? It bothered me. I believed that I had a better-than-average knowledge of the civil war in Nicaragua, having religiously followed the Iran-Contra hearings on television. I would videotape them while I was at work and watch them late into the night, marvelling the next morning at how wretchedly the newspapers were covering the story.

Like most Americans, I knew the Contras had been a creation of the CIA, the darlings of the Reagan Right, made up largely of the vanquished followers of deposed Nicaraguan dictator Anastasio Somoza and his brutal army, the National Guard. But drug trafficking? Surely, I thought, if there had been some concrete evidence, it would have stuck in my mind. Maybe I was confusing it with something else.

During a break, I went to the restroom and bumped into Assistant U.S. Attorney Hall. Just in case he and the FBI really did think I was Coral's hit man, I introduced myself as a reporter. Hall eyed me cautiously.

"The big papers stayed as far away from this issue as they could. It was like they didn't want to know."

"Why would the *Mercury News* be interested in this case?" he asked. "You should have been here two years ago. This is old stuff now."

I considered tap dancing around his question. Normally I didn't tell people what I was working on, because then they didn't know what not to say. But I decided to hit Hall with it head-on and see what kind of reaction I got. It would probably be the last thing he'd expect to hear.

"I'm not really doing a story on this case. I'm looking into one of the witnesses. A man named Blandón. Am I pronouncing the name correctly?"

Hall appeared surprised. "What about him?"

"About his selling cocaine for the Contras."

Hall leaned back slightly, folded his arms, and gave me a quizzical smile. "Who have you been talking to?"

"Actually, I've been reading. And I was curious to know what you made of his testimony about selling drugs for the Contras in L.A. Did you believe him?"

"Well, yeah, but I don't know how you could absolutely confirm it. I mean, I don't know what to tell you," he said with a slight laugh. "The CIA won't tell me anything."

I jotted down his remark. "Oh, you've asked them?"

"Yeah, but I never heard anything back. Not that I expected to. But that's all ancient history. You're really doing a story about that?"

"I don't know if I'm doing a story at all," I said. "At this point, I'm just trying to see if there is one. Do you know where Blandón is these days?"

"Not a clue."

That couldn't be true, I thought. How could he *not* know? He was one of the witnesses against Rafael Corñejo. "From what I heard," I told him, "he's a pretty significant witness in your case here. He hasn't disappeared, has he? He is going to testify?"

Hall's friendly demeanor changed. "We're not at all certain about that."

Pursuing the investigation

When I got back to Sacramento, I called my editor at the main office in San Jose, Dawn Garcia, and filled her in on the day's events. Dawn was a former investigative reporter from the *San Francisco Chronicle* and had been the *Mercury*'s state editor for several years, overseeing our bureaus in Los Angeles, San Francisco, and Sacramento. We had a good working relationship and had broken a number of award-winning stories. Unlike many editors I'd worked with, Dawn could size up a story's news value fairly quickly.

I read her several portions of Blandón's grand jury testimony.

"Weren't there some stories about this back in the 1980s?" she asked.

"See, that's what I thought. I remember something, but I can't place the source."

"Maybe the Iran-Contra hearings?"

"I don't think so," I said. "I followed those hearings pretty closely. I don't remember anything about drug trafficking."

(Dawn's memory, it turned out, was better than mine. During one part of Oliver North's congressional testimony in July 1987, two men from Baltimore had jumped up in the audience with a large banner reading, "Ask about the cocaine smuggling." The men began shouting questions—"What about the cocaine dealing that the U.S. is paying for? Why don't you ask questions about drug deliveries?"—as they were dragged from the room by the police.)

"So, what do you think?" she asked, editorese for "Is there a story here and how long will it take to get it?"

"I don't know. I'd like to spend a little time looking into it at least. Hell, if his testimony is true, it could be a pretty good story. The Contras were selling coke in L.A.? I've never heard that one before."

She mulled it over for a moment before agreeing. "It's not like there's a lot going on in Sacramento right now," she said. That was true enough. The sun-baked state capital was entering its summertime siesta, when triple-digit temperatures sent solons adjourning happily to mountain or seashore locales.

With any luck, I was about to join them.

"I need to go down to San Diego for a couple days," I said. "Blandón testified that he was arrested down there in '92 for conspiracy, so there's probably a court file somewhere. He may be living down there, for all I know. Probably the quickest way to find out if what he was saying is true is to find him."

Dawn okayed the trip, and a few days later I was in balmy San Diego, squinting at microfiche in the clerk's office of the U.S. District Court. I found Blandón's case file within a few minutes.

He and six others, including his wife, had been secretly indicted May 5, 1992, for conspiring to distribute cocaine. He'd been buying wholesale quantities from suppliers and reselling it to other wholesalers. Way up on the food chain. According to the indictment, he'd been a trafficker for ten years, had clients nationwide, and had bragged on tape of selling other L.A. dealers between two and four tons of cocaine.

He was such a big-timer that the judge had ordered him and his wife held in jail without bail because they posed "a threat to the health and moral fiber of the community."

The file contained a transcript of a detention hearing, held to determine if the couple should be released on bail. Blandón's prosecutor, Assistant U.S. Attorney L.J. O'Neale, brought out his best ammo to persuade the judge to keep the couple locked up until trial. "Mr. Blandón's family was closely associated with the Somoza government that was overthrown in 1979," O'Neale said. Blandón had been partners with a Jairo Meneses in 764 kilos of cocaine that had been seized in Nicaragua in 1991, O'Neale claimed, and he also owned hotels and casinos in Nicaragua with Meneses. He had a house in Costa Rica. He had a business in Mexico, relatives in Spain, phony addresses all over the United States, and "unlimited access to money."

"He is a large-scale cocaine trafficker and has been for a long time," O'Neale argued. Given the amount of cocaine he'd sold, O'Neale said, Blandón's minimum mandatory punishment was "off the charts"—life plus a $4 million fine—giving him plenty of incentive to flee the country.

"When I was trying to tell Congress [about the Contras selling drugs in L.A.], I was getting death threats."

Blandón's lawyer, Brad Brunon, confirmed the couple's close ties to Somoza and produced a photo of them at a wedding reception with *El Presidente* and his spouse. That just showed what fine families they were from, he said. The accusations in Nicaragua against Blandón, Brunon argued, were "politically motivated because of Mr. Blandón's activities with the Contras in the early 1980s."

Damn, here it is again. His own lawyer says he was working for the Contras.

Brunon argued that the government had no case against his client, and no right to keep him in jail until the trial. "There is not the first kilogram of cocaine that had been seized in this case," Brunon said. "What you have are accusations from a series of informants." But the judge didn't see it that way. While allowing Chepita to post bond, he ordered Danilo held without bail.

From the docket sheet, I could see that the case had never gone to trial. Everyone had pleaded out, starting with Blandón. Five months after his arrest, he pleaded guilty to conspiracy, and the charges against his wife were dropped. After that, his fugitive codefendants were quickly arrested and pleaded guilty. But they all received extremely short sentences. One was even put on unsupervised probation.

A suspicious case

I didn't get it. If O'Neale had such a rock-solid case against a major drug-trafficking ring, why were they let off so easily? People did more time for burglary. Even Blandón, the ringleader, only got forty-eight months, and from the docket sheet it appeared that was later cut almost in half.

As I read on, I realized that Blandón was already back on the streets—totally unsupervised. No parole. Free as a bird. He'd walked out of jail September 19, 1994, on the arm of an INS agent, Robert Tellez. He'd done twenty-eight months for ten years of cocaine trafficking.

The last page of the file told me why. It was a motion filed by U.S. Attorney O'Neale, asking the court to unseal Blandón's plea agreement and a couple of internal Justice Department memorandums. "During the course of this case, defendant Oscar Danilo Blandón cooperated with and rendered substantial assistance to the United States," O'Neale wrote. At the government's request, his jail sentence had been secretly cut twice. O'Neale then persuaded the judge to let Blandón out of jail completely, telling the court he was needed as a full-time paid informant for the U.S. Department of Justice. Since he'd be undercover, O'Neale wrote, he couldn't very well have probation agents checking up on him. He was released on unsupervised probation.

All of this information had once been secret, I noticed, but since Blandón was going to testify in a case in northern California (the Corñejo case, I presumed), O'Neale had to have the plea agreement and all the records relating to his sentence reductions unsealed and turned over to defense counsel.

I walked back to my hotel convinced that I was on the right track. Now there were two separate sources saying—in court—that Blandón was involved with the Contras and had been selling large amounts of cocaine in Los Angeles. And when the government finally had a chance to put him away forever, it had opened up the cell doors and let him walk. I needed to find Blandón. I had a million questions only he could answer.

I began calling the defense attorneys involved in the 1992 conspiracy case, hoping one of them would know what had become of him. I struck out with every call. One of the lawyers was out of town. The rest of them remembered next to nothing about the case or their clients. "It was all over so quickly I barely had time to open a file," one said. The consensus was that once Blandón flipped, his compadres scrambled to get the best deal they could, and no one prepared for trial. Discovery had been minimal.

But one thing wasn't clear. What had the government gotten out of the deal that was worth giving Blandón and his crew such an easy ride?

O'Neale claimed he'd given information about a murder in the Bay Area, but from what I could see from his DEA and FBI interviews, he'd merely told the government that the man had been murdered—something the police already knew.

Back in Sacramento, I did some checking on the targets of the 1994 grand jury investigation—the Meneses family—and again my tipster's description proved accurate, perhaps even understated. I found a 1991 story from the *San Francisco Chronicle* and a 1986 *San Francisco Examiner* piece that strongly suggested that Meneses, too, had been dealing cocaine for the Contras during the 1980s. One of the stories described him as the "king of cocaine in Nicaragua" and the Cali cartel's representative there. The *Chronicle* story mentioned that a U.S. Senate investigation had run across him in connection with the Contras and allegations of cocaine smuggling.

That must have been where I heard about this Contra drug stuff before, I decided. A congressional hearing.

At the California State Library's Government Publications Section, I scoured the CIS indices, which catalog congressional hearings by topic and witness name. Meneses wasn't listed, but there had been a series of hearings back in 1987 and 1988, I saw, dealing with the issue of the Contras and cocaine: a subcommittee of the Senate Foreign Relations Committee, chaired by Senator John Kerry of Massachusetts.

For the next six days I sat with rolls of dimes at a microfiche printer in the quiet wood-paneled recesses of the library, reading and copying many of the 1,100 pages of transcripts and exhibits of the Kerry Committee hearings, growing more astounded each day. The committee's investigators had uncovered direct links between drug dealers and the Contras. They'd gotten into BCCI years before anyone knew what that banking scandal even was. They'd found evidence of Manuel Noriega's involvement with drugs—years before the invasion. Many of the Kerry Committee witnesses, I noted, later became U.S. Justice Department witnesses against Noriega.

Kerry and his staff had taken videotaped depositions from Contra leaders who acknowledged receiving drug profits, with the apparent knowledge of the CIA. The drug dealers had admitted—under oath—giving money to the Contras, and had passed polygraph tests. The pilots had admitted flying weapons down and cocaine and marijuana back, landing in at least one instance at Homestead Air Force Base in Florida. The exhibits included U.S. Customs reports, FBI reports, internal Justice Department memos. It almost knocked me off my chair.

It was all there in black and white. Blandón's testimony about selling cocaine for the Contras in L.A. wasn't some improbable fantasy. This could have actually happened.

Contacting the attorney

I called Jack Blum, the Washington, D.C., attorney who'd headed the Kerry investigation, and he confirmed that Norwin Meneses had been an early target. But the Justice Department, he said, had stonewalled the committee's requests for information and he had finally given up trying to obtain the records, moving on to other, more productive areas. "There was a lot of weird stuff going on out on the West Coast, but after our experiences with Justice . . . we mainly concentrated on the cocaine coming into the East."

"Why is it that I can barely remember this?" I asked. "I mean, I read the papers every day."

"It wasn't in the papers, for the most part. We laid it all out, and we were trashed," Blum said. "I've got to tell you, there's a real problem with the press in this town. We were totally hit by the leadership of the administration and much of the congressional leadership. They simply turned around and said, 'These people are crazy. Their witnesses are full of shit. They're a bunch of drug dealers, drug addicts, don't listen to them.' And they dumped all over us. It came from every direction and every corner. We were even dumped on by the Iran-Contra Committee. They wouldn't touch this issue with a ten-foot pole."

"There had to have been some reporters who followed this," I protested. "Maybe I'm naive, but this seems like a huge story to me."

Blum barked a laugh. "Well, it's nice to hear someone finally say that, even if it is ten years later. But what happened was, our credibility was questioned, and we were personally trashed. The administration and some people in Congress tried to make us look like crazies, and to some degree it worked. I remember having conversations with reporters in which they would say, 'Well, the administration says this is all wrong.' And I'd say, 'Look, the guy is going to testify to X, Y, and Z. Why don't you cover the fucking hearing instead of coming to me with what the administration says?' And they'd say, 'Well, the guy is a drug dealer. Why should I do that?' And I used to say this regularly: 'Look, the minute I find a Lutheran minister or priest who was on the scene when they were delivering 600 kilos of cocaine at some air base in Contra-land, I'll put him on the stand, but until then, you take what you can get.' The big papers stayed as far away from this issue as they could. It was like they didn't want to know."

There were two reporters, Blum said, who'd pursued the Contra drug story—Robert Parry and Brian Barger of the Associated Press—but they'd run into the same problems. Their stories were either trashed or ignored. There were also two reporters in Costa Rica—a *New York Times* stringer named Martha Honey and her husband, Tony Avirgan, an ABC cameraman, who had gone after the story as well, he said. Honey and Avirgan wound up being set up on phony drug charges in Costa Rica, spied on in the States by the FBI and former CIA agents, smeared, and ruined financially.

"I know Bob Parry is still here in Washington somewhere. He did the first stories and was one of the few who seemed to know what he was doing. You might want to talk to him," Blum suggested.

Contacting the reporter

Parry sounded slightly amused when I called him in Virginia. "Why in the world would you want to go back into this?" he asked. I told him of my discoveries about Meneses and Blandón, and the latter's cocaine sales in Los Angeles. I wondered if he or anyone else had ever reported this before.

"Not that I'm aware of," Parry said. "We never really got into where it was going once the cocaine arrived in the United States. Our stories dealt mainly with the Costa Rican end of things. This is definitely a new angle. You think you can show it was being sold in L.A.?"

"Yeah, I do. Well, one of the guys has even testified to it before a grand jury. But this is an area I've never done any reporting on before so I guess what I'm looking for is a little guidance," I told him. "Have you got any suggestions?"

There was a short silence on the other end of the phone. "How well do you get along with your editors?" Parry finally asked.

"Fine. Why do you ask?"

"Well, when Brian and I were doing these stories we got our brains beat out." Parry sighed. "People from the administration were calling our editors, telling them we were crazy, that our sources were no good, that we didn't know what we were writing about. The Justice Department was putting out false press releases saying there was nothing to this, that they'd investigated and could find no evidence. We were being attacked in the *Washington Times*. The rest of the Washington press corps sort of pooh-poohed the whole thing, and no one else would touch it. So we ended up being out there all by ourselves, and eventually our editors backed away completely, and I ended up quitting the AP. It was probably the most difficult time of my career."

"[Blandón's] been working for the government the whole damn time."

He paused. "Maybe things have changed, I don't know."

I was nonplussed. Bob Parry wasn't some fringe reporter. He'd won a Polk Award for uncovering the CIA assasination manual given to the Contras, and was the first reporter to expose Oliver North's illegal activities. But what he'd just described sounded like something out of a bad dream. I told him I didn't think that would be a problem at the *Mercury*. I'd done some controversial stories before, but the editors had stood by them, and we'd won some significant awards. I felt good about the paper, I told him.

"One place you might try is the National Archives," Parry offered. "They're in the process of declassifying Lawrence Walsh's files, and I've found some pretty remarkable things over there. It's a long shot, but if I were you, I'd file a FOIA for the men you mentioned and see if anything turns up."

It *was* a long shot, but Parry's hunch paid off. My Freedom of Information Act request produced several important clues, among them a 1986 FBI report about Blandón that alluded to a police raid and reported that Blandón's attorney, Brad Brunon, had called the L.A. County Sheriff's Office afterward and claimed that the CIA had "winked" at Blandón's activities. I also obtained 1987 FBI interviews with a San Francisco Contra supporter, Dennis Ainsworth, in which he told of his discovery that Norwin Meneses and a Contra leader named Enrique Bermúdez were dealing arms and drugs.

I tracked down Ainsworth and had another disconcerting conversation. You've got to be crazy, he said. He'd tried to alert people to this ten years ago, and it had ruined his life. "Nobody in Washington wanted to look at this. Republican, Democrat, nobody. They wanted this story buried and anyone who looked any deeper into it got buried along with it," Ainsworth said. "You're bringing up a very old nightmare. You have no idea what you're touching on here, Gary. No idea at all."

"I think I've got a pretty good idea," I said.

"Believe me," he said patiently, "you don't understand. I almost got killed. I had friends in Central America who were killed. There was a Mexican reporter who was looking into one end of this, and he wound up dead. So don't pretend that you know."

"If the Contras were selling drugs in L.A., don't you think people should know that?"

Ainsworth laughed. "L.A.? Meneses was selling it all over the country! Listen, he ran one of the major distributions in the U.S. It wasn't just L.A. He was national. And he was totally protected."

"I think that's the kind of thing the public needs to know about," I told him. "And that's why I need your help. You know a lot more about this topic than I do."

He was unmoved. "Look, when I was trying to tell Congress, I was getting death threats. And you're asking, you know, if I'm Jewish, would I like to go back and spend another six months in Dachau? Leave this alone. Take my advice. You can go on and write a lot of other things and maybe win a Pulitzer Prize, but all you're going to be after this is over is a persona non grata. Please. Everyone's forgotten about this and moved on with their lives."

A few days later I got a call from Corñejo's girlfriend. My one chance to hook up with Blandón had just fallen through. "He isn't going to be testifying at Rafael's trial after all," she told me. "Rafael's attorney won his motion to have the DEA and FBI release the uncensored files, and the U.S. attorney decided to drop him as a witness rather than do that. Can you believe it? He was one of the witnesses they used to get the indictment against Rafael, and now they're refusing to put him on the stand."

I hung up the phone in a funk. Without him, I didn't have much to go on. But there was always his boss—this Meneses fellow. Getting to him was a tougher nut to crack, but worth a shot. The girlfriend said she thought he was in jail in Nicaragua, and the *Chronicle* clip I'd found noted that he'd been arrested there in 1991. Maybe, I hoped, the Nicaraguans locked their drug lords up longer than we did. I was put in touch with a freelance reporter in Managua, Georg Hodel, an indefatigable Swiss journalist who spoke several languages and had covered Nicaragua during the war. He taught college journalism classes, knew his way around the Nicaraguan government, and had sources everywhere. Better yet, with his Swiss-German-Spanish accent, it was like talking to Peter Lorre. I persuaded Dawn to hire Georg as a stringer, and he set off to find Meneses.

Meanwhile, the San Diego attorney who had been out of town when I was looking for Blandón returned my call. Juanita Brooks had represented Blandón's friend and codefendant, a Mexican millionaire named Sergio Guerra. Another lawyer in her firm had defended Chepita Blandón. She knew quite a bit about the couple.

"You don't happen to know where he is these days, do you?"

"No, but I can tell you where he'll be in a couple of months. Here in San Diego. Entirely by coincidence, I have a case coming up where he's the chief prosecution witness against my client."

"You're kidding," I said. "What case is this?"

"It's a pretty big one. Have you ever heard of someone named Freeway Ricky Ross?"

Indeed I had. I'd run across him while researching the asset forfeiture series in 1993. "He's one of the biggest crack dealers in L.A.," I said.

"That's what they say," Brooks replied. "He and my client and a couple others were arrested in a DEA reverse sting last year and Blandón is the CI [confidential informant] in the case."

"How did Blandón get involved with crack dealers?"

"I don't have a lot of details, because the government has been very protective of him. They've refused to give us any discovery so far," Brooks said. "But from what I understand, Blandón used to be one of Ricky Ross's sources back in the 1980s, and I suppose he played off that friendship."

My mind was racing. Blandón, the Contra fund-raiser, had sold cocaine to the biggest crack dealer in South Central L.A.? That was too much.

"Are you sure about this?"

"I wouldn't want you to quote me on it," she said, "but, yes, I'm pretty sure. You can always call Alan Fenster, Ross's attorney, and ask him. I'm sure he knows."

Fenster was out, so I left a message on his voice mail, telling him I was working on a story about Oscar Danilo Blandón Reyes and wanted to interview him. When I got back from lunch, I found a message from Fenster waiting. It said: "Oscar who?"

More damaging information

My heart sank. I'd suspected it was a bum lead, but I'd been keeping my fingers crossed anyway. I should have known; that would have been too perfect. I called Fenster back to thank him for his time, and he asked what kind of a story I was working on. I told him—the Contras and cocaine.

"I'm curious," he said. "What made you think this Oscar person was involved in Ricky's case?"

I told him what Brooks had related, and he gasped.

"He's the informant? Are you serious? No wonder those bastards won't give me his name!" Fenster began swearing a blue streak.

"Forgive me," he said. "But if you only knew what kind of bullshit I've been going through to get that information from those sons of bitches, and then some reporter calls me up from San Jose and he knows all about him, it just makes me—"

"Your client didn't tell you his name?"

"He didn't know it! He only knew him as Danilo, and then he wasn't even sure that was his real name. You and Ricky need to talk. I'll have him call you." He hung up abruptly.

Ross called a few hours later. I asked him what he knew about Blandón. "A lot," he said. "He was almost like a godfather to me. He's the one who got me going."

"Was he your main source?"

"He was. Everybody I knew, I knew through him. So really, he could be considered as my only source. In a sense, he was."

"When was this?"

"Eighty-one or '82. Right when I was getting going."

Damn, I thought. That was right when Blandón said he started dealing drugs.

"Would you be willing to sit down and talk to me about this?" I asked.

"Hell, yeah. I'll tell you anything you want to know."

At the end of September 1995 I spent a week in San Diego, going through the files of the Ross case, interviewing defense attorneys and prosecutors, listening to undercover DEA tapes. I attended a discovery hearing and watched as Fenster and the other defense lawyers made another futile attempt to find out details about the government's informant, so they could begin preparing their defenses. Assistant U.S. Attorney O'Neale refused to provide a thing. They'd get what they were entitled to, he promised, ten days before trial.

"See what I mean?" Fenster asked me on his way out. "It's like the trial in *Alice in Wonderland*."

I spent hours with Ross at the Metropolitan Correctional Center. He knew nothing of Blandón's past, I discovered. He had no idea who the Contras were or whose side they were on. To him, Danilo was just a nice guy with a lot of cheap dope.

"What would you say if I were to tell you that he was working for the Contras, selling cocaine to help them buy weapons and supplies?" I asked.

Ross goggled. "And they put me in jail? I'd say that was some fucked-up shit there. They say I sold dope all over, but man, I *know* he done sold ten times more than me. Are you being straight with me?"

I told him I had documents to prove it. Ross just shook his head and looked away.

"He's been working for the government the whole damn time," he muttered.

14

The CIA Has Not Been Involved in Drug Trafficking

Central Intelligence Agency

The Central Intelligence Agency (CIA) is the coordinating agency for U.S. federal intelligence activities. The agency is responsible for collecting and analyzing information on foreign nations for the use of the president in policy decisions.

A thorough investigation conducted by a CIA investigations staff determined that the CIA was not involved in smuggling cocaine into Los Angeles in the 1980s as a way of funding the Nicaraguan Contras. On the contrary, the staff found that the CIA had no connection with any of the drug traffickers alleged to have a relationship with the agency. In addition, the report found that the drug traffickers were in fact selling drugs for personal profit, not to aid the Contras in their attempt to overthrow the ruling Sandinista regime. Moreover, evidence indicated that the CIA did not attempt to influence the outcome of the drug traffickers' trials.

In August 1996, the *San Jose Mercury News* published the "Dark Alliance" series of articles alleging, among other things, that cocaine was "virtually unobtainable in black neighborhoods before members of the CIA's army"—the Nicaraguan Contras—started bringing it into South Central Los Angeles in the 1980s. The articles stated that Danilo Blandon, identified as a former Contra leader and a supplier of cocaine to Los Angeles drug dealer Ricky Ross, had testified in court that his cocaine profits supported the Contras, and that Blandon's attorney had concluded that Blandon was selling cocaine for CIA.

The articles also reported that major narcotics trafficker Norwin Meneses had a relationship with the Contras, that CIA or others had hampered the criminal investigation of Meneses and that a relative of Meneses alleged that Meneses had financed the Contras. The articles also claimed that an associate of Blandon, Ronald Lister, was connected to CIA.

Further, the articles claimed that Carlos Cabezas, who had been convicted in a 1983 San Francisco drug prosecution known as "The Frogman

From the *Report of Investigation Concerning Allegations of Connections Between CIA and the Contras in Cocaine Trafficking to the United States*, by the Central Intelligence Agency, Office of the Inspector General Investigations Staff, January 29, 1998.

Case," was connected to Meneses and that Cabezas had obtained cocaine from drug trafficker Horacio Pereira, who had contact with the Contras. Finally, the articles reported that funds that had been seized from Julio Zavala, a leader of the prosecuted drug ring, had been returned to him by the U.S. Attorney's Office because of Zavala's claim that the money belonged to the Contras.

The Office of Inspector General investigation

[Then] Director of Central Intelligence John Deutch asked the CIA Inspector General to investigate these allegations of connections between CIA, the Contras and drug trafficking. A 17-person team was formed to conduct the investigation and to work closely with the Department of Justice/Office of the Inspector General. The team reviewed 250,000 pages of documents and conducted over 365 interviews, most under oath, including current and former CIA employees, other current and former U.S. Government officials, as well as private citizens and foreign nationals. The principal individuals discussed in the *San Jose Mercury News* articles, including Ross, Blandon, Meneses, Lister, Zavala, and Cabezas, were among those interviewed. The Office of Inspector General interviews involved travel to four continents and throughout the United States.

Investigative findings: Ross, Blandon, Meneses, and Lister

Ricky Ross. There has never been any CIA relationship with Ricky Ross. Ross states that he provided no money to the Contras and had no contact with the Contras or CIA. Ross also denies that CIA or the Contras had anything to do with his drug trafficking.

Ross says he began dealing cocaine in 1979 or 1980 and learned to make "crack" in 1981 from another acquaintance in Los Angeles, not CIA. He met Blandon in 1983 and claims to have become the largest Los Angeles cocaine dealer before ever meeting Blandon. Ross claims to have purchased 100 kilograms of cocaine weekly from Blandon and 40 to 100 kilograms a week from another dealer, Ivan Torres. Ross says he obtained cocaine from Blandon until 1988 or 1989.

Ross says he believes that CIA was involved with Blandon. However, he says this belief is based solely on what he has learned from the media. Ross says he has no knowledge of any contacts between Blandon and CIA.

The [investigation] team reviewed 250,000 pages of documents and conducted over 365 interviews.

Danilo Blandon. There has never been any CIA relationship with Danilo Blandon, and CIA was unaware of Blandon until 1986 when he was arrested and reportedly claimed a CIA connection. At the request of the FBI, CIA checked its records at that time and found no information in its possession regarding Blandon.

Blandon says that he has never had any relationship with CIA, was never approached by the Contras to raise money by drug trafficking and did not provide millions of dollars to the Contras as has been alleged in the media. He recalls giving several thousand dollars to support the operating expenses of Contra sympathizers in California in the 1980s, and he recalls providing several thousand dollars, the use of two automobiles and accommodations in Costa Rica to Contra leader Eden Pastora on a personal basis.

Blandon says he met Norwin Meneses in 1981, and Meneses supplied him with cocaine to sell from then until 1983 when they had a dispute. Blandon says he met Ross in 1984, began selling him cocaine in 1985 and stopped in 1986. Blandon says he provided Ross as much as 50 kilograms at a time, but denies Ross' claim that he provided as much as 100 kilograms weekly.

There has never been any CIA relationship with [drug dealer] Danilo Blandon.

Norwin Meneses. There has never been any CIA relationship with Norwin Meneses. CIA records indicate that Meneses' name appeared on occasion in CIA intelligence reports regarding drug trafficking and that information was shared with U.S. law enforcement agencies. Meneses denies any contact or relationship with CIA.

Meneses says he was associated with the Contras, but denies he ever raised any money for Contra organizations through drug trafficking. He also says that he is not aware of any Contra involvement in drug trafficking. Meneses says that his only contribution to the Contras was an estimated $3,000 that he gave to a group of Contra sympathizers in California to support their administrative expenses between 1982 and 1984.

Ronald Lister. There has never been any CIA relationship with Ronald Lister despite any claims he may have made to the contrary. Lister says he has never been a CIA employee and was never asked by CIA to assist Blandon or the Contras in any way. Lister also says that he and Blandon engaged in their drug trafficking activities for personal profit and did not do so on behalf of CIA or the Contras.

Findings: The Frogman Case

In 1983, more than 50 individuals, including many Nicaraguans, were arrested in the San Francisco area for cocaine trafficking in what was known as "The Frogman Case." None of those who were arrested or charged had relationships with CIA, though a relative of one of them had a relationship with CIA until mid-1982. None claimed a Contra or a CIA connection at the time. Later, two of those arrested—Julio Zavala and Carlos Cabezas—claimed links to the Contras. Cabezas also later alleged that he engaged in cocaine trafficking to support the Contras.

Julio Zavala. In 1984, CIA became aware of The Frogman Case and Zavala when it was learned that representatives of the U.S. Attorney's Office in San Francisco were planning to travel to Costa Rica for the depositions of two Nicaraguans. The depositions had been requested by Zavala's lawyers.

The Nicaraguans who were to be deposed were members of Contra organizations and had provided letters attesting to the truthfulness of Zavala's claim that the approximately $36,000 that was seized when he was arrested belonged to the Contras. It appears that the letters were obtained through Zavala's wife's connections with family friends and not because he was active in any Contra group. In fact, the principal author of the letters was reportedly expelled from a Contra group when its leadership learned that he had done so and he could not explain the basis for his actions.

Based upon the information available to them at the time, CIA personnel reached the erroneous conclusion that one of the two individuals who was to be deposed was a former CIA asset. Subsequently, an attorney from the Agency's Office of General Counsel (OGC) met with the responsible U.S. Attorney (AUSA). CIA believed that the proposed depositions in Costa Rica might lead to a Contra support group in which it had an operational interest.

The AUSA already had discussed with Zavala's lawyer the possibility of returning the seized money rather than traveling to Costa Rica for the depositions, the purpose of which was ostensibly to establish who owned the money. The money, which may, in fact, have been profit from drug trafficking, was ultimately returned to Zavala.

None of those who were arrested or charged [in the Frogman drug case] had relationships with CIA.

A CIA cable, written by the OGC attorney who met with the AUSA, indicated that the $36,000 seized from Zavala was returned to Zavala at CIA's request. The AUSA, the former U.S. Attorney and others involved in the prosecution state, however, that the decision to return the money to Zavala was based on their own judgment as to whether the expense and effort of traveling to Costa Rica was necessary to prove their case and not on CIA's representations. Zavala was subsequently convicted and sentenced to prison.

Carlos Cabezas. Cabezas was arrested, convicted and sentenced in connection with The Frogman Case. Cabezas says that he began bringing cocaine into the United States in 1981 with Zavala, Troilo Sanchez and Horacio Pereira. According to Cabezas, Zavala had his own drug network, but also was part of a second network that sold cocaine for the Contras. Cabezas also claims he witnessed Pereira deliver money to a Contra member. However, Cabezas' drug associates in The Frogman Case, the FBI Special Agents who investigated The Frogman Case and U.S. Attorney's Office personnel who were responsible for the prosecution dispute these claims. They recall no evidence being developed during the extensive investigations of any connection between Cabezas and the Contras. Nor has any information been found to support Cabezas' subsequent claims that he had connections to the Contras or that he engaged in drug trafficking on behalf of the Contras.

Norwin Meneses. No information has been found to connect Meneses with The Frogman Case. Meneses says he was never part of the Zavala organization. Zavala and Cabezas confirm this assertion.

The CIA was not involved

Did CIA have any relationship or dealings with Ross, Blandon or Meneses? No information has been found to indicate that any past or present employee of CIA, or anyone acting on behalf of CIA, had any direct or indirect dealing with Ricky Ross, Oscar Danilo Blandon or Juan Norwin Meneses. Additionally, no information has been found to indicate that CIA had any relationship or contact with Ronald J. Lister or David Scott Weekly, the person Lister allegedly claimed was his CIA contact. No information has been found to indicate that any of these individuals was ever employed by CIA, or met by CIA employees or anyone acting on CIA's behalf.

Was the drug trafficking of Ross, Blandon or Meneses linked to CIA or Contra activities? No information has been found to indicate that Ross provided any money to any Contra group at any time, or that he had any contact or connection to the Contras or CIA.

No information has been found to indicate that the drug trafficking activities of Blandon and Meneses were motivated by any commitment to support the Contra cause or Contra activities undertaken by CIA.

Blandon and Meneses claim that they each donated between $3,000 and $40,000 to Contra sympathizers in Los Angeles. No information has been found to substantiate these claims. Moreover, no information has been found to indicate that Meneses or Blandon received any CIA or Contra support for their drug trafficking activities.

Blandon did have a personal relationship with Eden Pastora and provided him with financial assistance in the form of rent-free housing and two vehicles. Much of this assistance was provided to Pastora after he left the Contra movement.

Did CIA intervene or otherwise play a role in any investigative and judicial processes involving the drug trafficking activities of Ross, Blandon or Meneses? No information has been found to indicate that CIA hindered, or otherwise intervened in, the investigation, arrest, prosecution, or conviction of Ross, Blandon or Meneses. CIA shared what information it had—specifically on Meneses' 1979 drug trafficking in Nicaragua—with U.S. law enforcement entities when it was received and again when subsequently requested by the FBI.

No information has been found to indicate that CIA hindered, or otherwise intervened in, the investigation, arrest, prosecution, or conviction of [the drug traffickers].

Did any of the individuals who were arrested in "The Frogman Case" have any relationship with CIA? Were the drug trafficking activities of any of those individuals linked to the Contras? No information has been found to indicate that CIA or individuals acting on behalf of CIA had any relationship with Julio Zavala, Carlos Cabezas or others who were arrested or charged in connection with the 1983 Frogman Case, though a relative of one of them had a relationship with CIA until mid-1982.

No information has been found to indicate that Julio Zavala, Carlos

Cabezas or other Frogman Case defendants were connected to the Contras or that the Contras benefited from their drug trafficking activities. No information has been found to support Cabezas' claim that he provided financial assistance to the Contras from his drug trafficking activities. While two individuals who were active in the Contra movement wrote letters supporting Zavala's claim that seized money belonged to the Contras, it appears this was done through Zavala's wife's connections to old family friends and not because Zavala was active in the Contra movement.

Was CIA involved in the investigation of The Frogman Case? No information has been found to indicate that CIA or anyone acting on behalf of CIA was involved in the criminal investigation of Julio Zavala and his associates, though a relative of one of those arrested or charged did have a relationship with CIA until mid-1982.

To what extent and why did CIA become involved in the prosecution of The Frogman Case? CIA did make contact with prosecutors in the Zavala prosecution in order to protect what CIA believed was an operational equity, i.e., a Contra support group in which it had an operational interest. A CIA cable indicates that approximately $36,000 seized from Zavala at the time of his arrest was returned to Zavala—based on the claim they were Contra funds—by the prosecutors at CIA's request. However, the prosecutors state that the decision to return Zavala's money was based on other considerations, not CIA's representations, and that there was no evidentiary value to retaining the money. In any event, the actions taken by CIA to have the cash returned did not appear to be intended to influence the outcome of Zavala's trial, which resulted in his conviction.

15

The CIA Is Seriously Flawed

Ted Gup

Ted Gup, a former investigative reporter for the Washington Post *and* Time, *has covered the U.S. intelligence community for the past twenty years.*

The CIA should be radically reformed or abolished. As evidenced by the September 11, 2001, terrorist attacks on America, the CIA is incapable of responding to modern threats to America's national security. The agency still uses the information-gathering techniques that it utilized during the Cold War, but these techniques are no longer effective because America no longer faces just one major enemy and its sphere of influence. The United States must now respond to multiple threats from various rogue nations and the individual terrorists those nations harbor. An additional problem is that new agency recruits are unqualified and unwilling to infiltrate Middle Eastern nations, from which the most serious terrorist threats arise. Rather than openly admit its mistakes and try to change, the CIA blames others for its failures.

A few years back, a callow new recruit to the CIA, aspiring to be a paramilitary officer, asked a grizzled veteran of clandestine operations if he could accompany him on an undercover mission to the Middle East. He was looking for a mentor, someone to give him an advanced course in the tradecraft of espionage. The old pro, then in his late 50s, looked at the wide-eyed case officer and asked him to smile. The younger agent was puzzled, but obliged, revealing what the more seasoned operative estimated to be some $20,000 worth of American orthodontics.

"Every time you open your mouth," he chided the young man, "you will be telling people where you come from. You can make that trip, but we will have to knock out a few teeth and things like that." The recruit's ardor for the assignment instantly paled. And so ended a partnership even before it began.

It was a brief exchange, but one revealing of innumerable frailties in the CIA's campaign against terrorism. It may be unfair to suggest that the CIA was negligent in failing to foil the September 11, 2001, terrorist attacks, and even the agency's harshest critics must recognize the numbing

From "Clueless in Langley," by Ted Gup, *Mother Jones*, January/February 2002. Copyright © 2002 by Mother Jones Magazine. Reprinted with permission.

obstacles involved in penetrating terrorist cells. But it is not unfair to ask whether the vaunted Central Intelligence Agency is up to the task of fighting terrorism.

Too late for the CIA?

Like the young recruit who hoped to accompany the veteran into the field, the CIA is earnest enough but arguably so ill equipped and ill suited that nothing short of fundamentally altering its identity—the bureaucratic equivalent of knocking out its front teeth—would suffice. In short, it is time to consider either fundamentally overhauling the agency or getting rid of it entirely. We quite simply may no longer be able to entrust it with the vital mission of collecting and analyzing the intelligence upon which the nation's survival could depend.

In some ways it may be too late for the CIA to adapt to the current crisis. Locked in a past wholly defined by the Cold War, the agency has struggled to shed its historical roots and to become something that it is not and never has been—agile, prescient, and proactive. Already past are many of the opportunities to make the sort of long-term investments in on-the-ground intelligence that might have helped thwart today's terrorists. It is only a failed intelligence community that invokes the defense of hindsight being 20/20.

It is time to consider either fundamentally overhauling the agency or getting rid of it entirely.

Back in 1947, when the CIA was created out of the remnants of World War II's Office of Strategic Services, its mission was to fight Communism. Its enemies were Moscow and Beijing. Decade after decade, the agency viewed every conflict in much the same light, as one played out between superpower proxies. Today it remains enslaved to this Cold War legacy, with both its structure and vision predicated on a world divided into states and spheres of influence. Notwithstanding its recognition of transnational issues—terrorism, weapons proliferation, drugs, crime—many of its officials and operatives continue to view the world even as a child views a grade-school globe with neatly drawn borders. They speak of state-sponsored terrorism, unable to imagine terrorists without such support. Only now are they discovering that it may be the terrorists who support the state, and that states harboring terrorists may themselves be held hostage by fear of extremism. Agency analysts who comb through news reports, government documents, and other open-source intelligence on individual nations can ascertain the gross national product of Yemen or the wheat crop in Ukraine, but they will not crack the nut of terrorism.

To its credit, the CIA has tried to overcome its bureaucratic and hierarchical burdens. As far back as 1986 it created the Counter-Terrorism Center, a major effort to try to break out of the Cold War mold. Composed of representatives from numerous organizations, including the CIA, the Pentagon, and the FBI, the center represents the first time the agency has allowed analysts, operatives, and techies to work side by side. But the unit has been riddled with conflict, and it remains a component, albeit an ever-growing one, within the antiquated structure that predates it.

In other ways, too, the Cold War mind-set hampers the CIA's efforts to pursue and prosecute terrorists. Too many case officers are still being placed under cover at embassies around the world, a system reminiscent of the days when the burglars and break-in artists of Langley, [Virginia, where the CIA's headquarters is located] stole secrets from foreign offices in "black bag" jobs. But few terrorists have their encampments in big cities, much less capitals—an obvious problem that remains uncorrected, in part, because case officers are reluctant to move out of the cities and into the bush. The ranks of covert operatives are filled with erudite young men and women who enlist to experience foreign cultures. Eating dust and lying low in godforsaken outposts is not high on anyone's list.

Personnel problems

Forty years ago, few agents gave serious thought to personal comforts. But such veterans are largely gone. When the Cold War ended, so did much of Langley's sense of purpose. Thousands of seasoned operatives and analysts retired, and with them went a deep reservoir of experience and commitment.

The old boys may have a rose-tinted view of the past, but it does seem to many of them that today's recruits are as concerned with retirement and health benefits as with the agency's mission. On September 26, 2001, President George W. Bush paid a visit to Langley and commiserated with agency employees for the long hours they had endured. He spoke of "sleeping on the floor, eating cold pizza," as if that were the ultimate sacrifice. In the caves of Afghanistan, such conditions would be a step up.

No one seemed more blindsided by the events of September 11 than the CIA. Until that day, the agency had been strutting its stuff, suggesting in background briefings and off-the-record comments that the terrorists were on the run. It cited a steady decline in attacks, interpreting the prolonged silence as evidence of capitulation or fear, seemingly oblivious to the idea that the silence was that of a plan coming together.

An agency that lives in the realm of deception and secrecy had indulged in a campaign to enhance its public image. It had a longtime veteran of covert operations, Chase Brandon, assigned to be a liaison with Hollywood, to consult on the scripts of prime-time programs such as *The Agency* and *24*. Authors like Tom Clancy who portray the CIA in a favorable light were given wide access, while more critical observers found the door still closed.

An over-reliance on technology

All the while, the agency was not only hemorrhaging experienced operatives, but increasingly coming to rely on technology as the principal element of espionage. Human intelligence—the network of spies on the ground—was allowed to degrade steadily. To the fore came satellite imagery and the National Security Agency's capacity to intercept communications. High-tech spying had proved effective against foreign states during the Cold War. Against terrorism, its value was dubious at best.

Overhead satellites are fine for tracking troop movements, but a fast-moving cell of terrorists, or a training camp consisting of little more than tents and rifle ranges, can easily elude an eye in the sky. Reading a license plate from outer space is great in securing funds for more "birds," but it is worthless without a footprint on the ground.

And those who monitor intercepts can easily be outwitted. Islamic terrorist Osama bin Laden and others appear to have used the United States' eavesdropping capacity to send intelligence agencies on wild-goose chases. In addition, the crushing volume of data often precludes analysts' ability to find the key messages until after the fact—after the attack. Such technology may be useful as a tool in gathering evidence, but it comes as little comfort to the bereaved.

Today's recruits are as concerned with retirement and health benefits as with the agency's mission.

In the end, the most productive intelligence on terrorists will come from human spies on the ground. But here, too, the CIA has been woefully slow off the mark. It has an abundance of case officers fluent in French and German and Russian, but, as we now know all too well, few who speak Arabic, Farsi, or Pashto and could slip unnoticed into a street in the Middle East. For two decades it has been clear that this is a region from which much trouble comes, yet the agency failed to aggressively train and prepare a cadre of covert operatives to penetrate the ranks of radical Islamic terrorists. Infiltrating terrorist cells is as difficult as it is dangerous—but that is the mission of an intelligence agency.

The blame game

For decades the CIA has been wrestling with its own demons. Publicly, it has made excuses, blaming others for its inability to frustrate the plans of terrorists. In 1983, the U.S. Embassy in Beirut, Lebanon, was bombed. Six months later, a car bomb brought down the Marine barracks there. A government commission later blamed the CIA for failing to sniff out the plan in advance. But former CIA director Stansfield Turner defended the agency in his book *Secrecy and Democracy*.

"It was unreasonable," he wrote, "to expect the CIA to have anticipated this particular threat far enough in advance to have placed an agent in every terrorist organization. Spies cannot be recruited overnight. A suitable candidate must be identified, his friendship and trust nurtured over weeks and months until he is willing to work for us, an opportunity found to insert him in the organization we want to learn about, and enough time allowed him to gain the trust of that organization. In Lebanon the CIA would have had to elevate terrorism to a very high priority perhaps a year or more before the actual attack."

Exactly. Turner sounds as though the idea of planning for something a year or more in advance is unreasonable. As the September 11 attacks made clear, terrorists do not find it unreasonable. American intelligence still operates on a kind of ATM mentality: put the card in and get the information out. It would seem that one edge the terrorists possess is that of patience.

No sooner had the smoke cleared on September 11 than the CIA began to argue that it couldn't do its job because there were too many morals and too few dollars. Officials once more chafed against the ban on assassinations of foreign leaders, first issued by President Gerald Ford in 1976, as if it had somehow encumbered the intelligence community's work. The fact is that the CIA was never much good at killing foreign leaders, and even before the ban it failed, and failed miserably. The individual who has been targeted by the agency more often, and in more ways, than any other remains the longest-serving sovereign in the hemisphere: [Cuba's premier] Fidel Castro.

There is also not a small amount of hypocrisy in suggesting that U.S. actions have been constrained by any such ban. No one really doubted who the target was when Air Force planes bombed [Libyan head of state] Muammar Gadhafi's personal bunker in 1986, killing his adopted daughter, or when [former president] George Bush Sr. sent missiles raining down on [Iraqi president] Saddam Hussein's palaces. Osama bin Laden was still alive three years after being implicated in the 1998 bombings of two U.S. embassies, not because of any ban on assassinations, but because the CIA had no idea where he was.

Then there's the agency complaint about the Torricelli principle (named for Senator Robert Torricelli of New Jersey, who introduced it in 1995), which prohibits field agents from bringing drug dealers, murderers, and other miscreants on board without authorization from Langley. Granted, espionage is not for Boy Scouts: "If you're going after the rats, you have to get down in the sewers," as one former operative puts it. But have we forgotten so quickly the lowlifes, from rogue contras [who attempted a military coup against the established government in Nicaragua in the 1980s] to the likes of former Nicaraguan leader Manuel Noriega, who were used and supported by the CIA in Central America? Perhaps field agents have been reluctant to put forward the names of some sordid candidates, but that may not be a bad thing: Historically, the CIA's lack of discretion in choosing its allies has surely caused as many problems as it has solved.

Finally, of course, the CIA blames the press, members of Congress, and anyone who dares to speak of that which it has stamped secret. In the fall of 2000, the agency's allies in Congress attempted to enact a secrecy law that would have sent anyone who disclosed a classified document to prison for three years. The proposal passed without hearings or debate and might well have won President Bill Clinton's signature had it not been for a coalition of influential journalists who lobbied against it.

Leaks

More recently the administration, with support from the CIA, has attempted to severely limit the number of members of congressional intelligence committees who are cleared for classified briefings. What infuriated officials was the leaked warning, first disclosed in a congressional briefing, that there was a 100 percent chance of further terrorist attacks against the United States, probably focusing on infrastructure like nuclear power plants or gas pipelines. Was that not something the public had a right to know?

Despite protestations to the contrary, what galls the CIA most is not that leaks damage national security, but rather that it can't keep its secrets secret. Adept at leaks that are self-serving, it brands as traitorous only those that contradict the party line. A federal agency known as the Information Security Oversight Office estimates that the CIA created some 3.5 million new secrets in 1999. If only one of them could have thwarted the September 11 attack.

To justify such obsessive secrecy, the agency often invokes the need to protect its "sources and methods"—the who and how of intelligence gathering. At headquarters in Langley, a volume known as the "Book of Honor" lists covert operatives killed in the line of duty. In half the cases, the operatives' identities are concealed, marked by anonymous stars. One of those stars represents Barbara Robbins, a 21-year-old CIA secretary killed by a car bomb in Saigon in 1965. The agency has suppressed her name despite appeals from her father to recognize her. It is a strange organization that can conceal the identity of a dead secretary for 35 years but cannot protect the lives of foreign agents imperiled by a CIA mole like Aldrich Ames. McGeorge Bundy, a former national security adviser, once observed, "If we guard our toothbrushes and diamonds with equal zeal, we will lose fewer toothbrushes and more diamonds." Small wonder John Deutch, who served as CIA director for two years in the Clinton administration, showed such contempt for secrecy as to view ultrasensitive materials on his unsecured home computer.

The agency failed to aggressively train and prepare a cadre of covert operatives to penetrate the ranks of radical Islamic terrorists.

The reality is that most agency secrets have less to do with genuine national security than with the expediencies of a bureaucracy. Marking a memo "Secret" gives it a certain cachet, makes it worthy of attention in the blizzard of paperwork that consumes government offices. No such stamp and it's dispatched to oblivion.

But such rampant secrecy creates a sclerotic agency incapable of fulfilling its most basic functions. In the air war against Yugoslavia in the 1990s, NATO ran out of targets and turned to the CIA for suggestions. The agency came up with what it said was the Federal Directorate of Supply and Procurement in Belgrade. Only after the structure was leveled and the bodies were counted was it discovered that the building was the Chinese Embassy. This was a fact well known to CIA analysts familiar with Belgrade; unfortunately, they had not been consulted.

So it was, too, when President Clinton sent a cruise missile into the Al Shifa pharmaceutical plant in Sudan in 1998 in retaliation for the embassy bombings in Kenya and Tanzania. Agency analysts had rushed to declare that soil tests had found proof positive that the plant was making chemical weapons. The proof turned out to be less than positive. "Al Shifa is what happens when you let the boys play with the toys," says one former spook.

The full extent of those earlier debacles could be cloaked in secrecy. The events of September 11 could not be. Today, the public's dissatisfaction with the intelligence community is palpable. One post-September 11 poll conducted by CBS News showed that some 56 percent of those surveyed considered the attack the largest single intelligence failure since Pearl Harbor.

Some now say that what the nation needs is a super-CIA, one placing the National Reconnaissance Office, the National Imagery and Mapping Agency, and the National Security Agency under the authority of Langley—a concentration of power and secrecy that should send shivers down the spines of civil libertarians.

The old-boy network

With such a track record, how is it that the CIA and its director, George Tenet, have not been subjected to more withering scrutiny from those charged with overseeing the intelligence behemoth? To explain why the agency has for years escaped criticism that might have led to corrective actions, one need only understand the workings of Washington's old-boy network. Ironically, the chief peril the CIA now faces comes not from having too many enemies, but too many friends.

Tenet has been at the head of the agency since Deutch left in December 1996. Prior to that, he held a top position at the National Security Council, and before that he served as the senior staffer on the Senate Select Committee on Intelligence, which oversees the CIA. His friends in the Senate are loath to put his toes to the fire.

Tenet also has little to fear from the House Select Committee: It is headed by Representative Porter Goss of Florida, who was a CIA operative before becoming a member of Congress. He has remained a faithful and steadfast cheerleader for Langley, though he admits that the agency's image could do with some polishing. Is it time to get rid of the CIA? "Now that's a fair question," Goss says. "If you ask me, 'Have you ever thought about changing the name, moving the building, putting up a different flag, calling it something else?' Yes, all of the above."

It is a strange organization that can conceal the identity of a dead secretary for 35 years but cannot protect the lives of foreign agents imperiled by a CIA mole.

Nor should one look to George W. Bush's White House for critical oversight of the CIA. The president is not about to take on an institution whose headquarters is named after his father, one of the agency's most popular former directors. "I've got a lot of confidence in [Tenet] and I've got a lot of confidence in the CIA," Bush declared during his September 2001 visit to Langley.

Of course, the most stinging irony is that until quite recently, when the CIA was asked to enumerate its successes, Afghanistan was near the top of the list. That was because arming and training the mujahedin provided the agency a direct opportunity to inflict harm on its prime adversary, the Soviet Union, and ultimately to drive the Red Army out of the country in a Vietnam-like debacle.

The ultimate confession of shortsightedness comes from former CIA director Robert M. Gates. In his 1996 book, *From the Shadows*, he writes: "Our mission was to push the Soviets out of Afghanistan. We expected post-Soviet Afghanistan to be ugly, but never considered that it would become a haven for terrorists operating worldwide." The key words: "never considered." Like American foreign policy itself, the agency has often been myopic, operating on the principle that the enemy of our enemy is our friend. In a world of complexity, it has promoted stopgap measures that often made lasting solutions even more elusive.

Today the CIA is hamstrung by its own sullied past. At home, critics suspect it of having had a hand in the assassination of John F. Kennedy, of introducing crack cocaine into South Central Los Angeles, and of a host of other conspiracies that remain utterly unproved. Overseas, its past shadows it from country to country and continent to continent, clouding America's moral standing and its ability to gather the kind of intelligence that the nation will need in the years ahead.

Americans have long viewed the CIA as a rogue agency, its errant missions the work of covert cowboys. The truth—that everything it did, good and bad, originated in the Oval Office with either a presidential directive or a wink and a nod—is less comforting. It means that we as a nation bear a measure of responsibility for its actions, and its failures. Whether the CIA is still capable of effectively serving the nation is a question that can no longer be ignored.

16

America Still Needs the CIA

George Tenet

George Tenet is director of the Central Intelligence Agency.

The CIA exists to gather information on foreign nations, analyze and synthesize that information to help the president make informed policy decisions, and provide warnings about major geopolitical transformations that threaten national security. Such activities have become even more important since the CIA was established in 1947. For one thing, the communications and information revolution has resulted in a massive increase in the amount of information available, and the president needs an agency to make sense of it. Moreover, the global proliferation of biological and nuclear weapons makes an agency that can obtain information about the weapons capabilities of America's enemies more important than ever. CIA agents accomplish these critical tasks on behalf of the American people every day at great risk to themselves simply for the love of their country.

You have chosen as your topic the question of whether America still needs the CIA. I think this is the first time I've ever been asked to keynote a conference where the stated objective is deciding whether I should bother coming into work in the morning.

You will doubtless hear many views on the CIA during this conference. In stating mine, let me break the suspense and say that my answer to your question—does America still need the CIA—is an unambiguous "yes." I imagine that is what you would expect to hear from me. But let me be equally clear about why I say it. In a nutshell, it flows from my conviction that the compelling factors behind the creation of the CIA are still present in the world that America must live in today.

The CIA was created by President Harry S. Truman as an insurance policy against the kind of surprise that caught America off guard in World War II [when Pearl Harbor was bombed by the Japanese in 1941]. He was also annoyed by the confused and conflicting nature of the reports landing on his desk from various departments. He wanted someone to make sense of them, someone who had no policy axe to grind and someone whose exclusive mission was to work for him, and to ensure that he was not taken off guard by dangerous developments overseas.

From "Does America Need the CIA? Global Intelligence Is a Critical Deterrent to Bad Actors," by George Tenet, *Vital Speeches*, January 15, 1998. Copyright © 1998 by City News Publishing Company, Inc. Reprinted with permission.

As I look at the world today, it is clear to me that the potential for dangerous surprise is as great as ever.

That is true whether I look at terrorist groups whose sole purpose is to harm American interests, the biological weapons that Iraqi president Saddam Hussein is still trying to build and to hide in Iraq, or the programs Iran has for building intermediate range missiles and nuclear weapons.

It is true when I look at the ethnic tensions that make life dangerous for U.S. forces in Bosnia, the build up of North Korean forces near the DMZ or the vast and unfinished transformations under way in countries with large nuclear arsenals, such as Russia and China.

What Americans expect from the CIA

Against that backdrop, we can debate whether or not CIA should exist, but I must tell you that I have no doubt about what the American people expect of us as long as we do. They want us to:

- Protect the lives of Americans everywhere.
- Protect our men and women in uniform and ensure that they dominate the battlefield whenever they are called and wherever they are deployed.
- They want us to protect Americans from threats posed by terrorists, drug traffickers or weapons of mass destruction.
- They want intelligence to arm our diplomats with critical insights and foreknowledge that can help them advance American interests and avert conflicts.
- They went us to focus not just on threats but also on opportunities—opportunities to act before danger becomes disaster and opportunities to create circumstances favorable to America's interests.
- They went us to track and give advance warning about major geopolitical transformations in the world.
- And, they want our reporting and analysis to add real value to what they already know about the toughest problems facing the United States.

To live up to these expectations, we need to do four things very well:

- We need to produce outstanding all-source analysis that is timely, prescient, and persuasive.
- We need to mount imaginative and sophisticated clandestine human and technical operations in order to get vital information our nation cannot get in any other way.
- We need to be vigilant on the counterintelligence front.
- And, we need to sharpen CIA's capacity to effectively employ covert action on those occasions when our nation's leaders conclude that an important aim can be achieved through no other means.

These are essentially the 4 core mission areas of our business that I do not believe can be replicated anyplace else in our government. It is against this backdrop, however, that we must address the key question of your conference because it is an important one. So let's talk about CIA:

- What does CIA bring to the table?
- Why is it important?
- What difference does it make?
- Is it an investment worth making?

- And perhaps most important, can the American people trust us to carry out our responsibilities in a manner consistent with the values of our democratic society?

If we cannot answer these questions in a compelling and thoughtful way, then we should not exist.

If we cannot prove to the President that we are making progress against the most difficult and enduring threats to our national security, then we should not exist.

If we cannot prove that we will attack these targets with the highest standards of professional integrity, professional performance and dispassionate objectivity, then again we should not exist.

I believe we will meet these tests and, at the end of the day, we in the business of intelligence must have the courage and foresight to understand that this is precisely the kind of dialogue we must have with the American people.

An evolving institution

For my part, I do not intend to spend a lot of time discussing the past. As in any endeavor, we must learn from the past and never shy away from confronting mistakes. But as I said in my confirmation hearings, my gaze is fixed on the future, and on the task of creating the best intelligence service for the 21st century. Moreover, focusing on the past assumes that the CIA of yesterday is necessarily going to be the CIA of tomorrow. The fact is, the CIA has been, and must continue to be, an evolving institution. Not only have our targets changed, but the way we go about our work has changed—in part because of the revolution in information and communications technology, and in part because of the vast amount of information which is now available to all of us.

In addition, our relationship to the rest of the federal government has changed. We are more transparent than we used to be to policymakers within the Executive branch, and more integrated into their decision making. There are detailed procedures for coordinating our activities outside the United States which ensure that the President receives the views of other departments and agencies with legitimate interests in these activities before he approves them.

The CIA's classic mission of separating fact from fiction and presenting analysis objectively has become only more important.

There also is intense scrutiny from the Congress, not only of our operational activities, but of our analysis as well. I dare say the CIA receives more oversight from the Congress than any other agency in the federal government. This is not a complaint. In fact, this oversight is our most vital and direct link to the American people, a source of strength that separates us from all other countries of the world.

So focusing on today, what do we bring to the table and what difference does it make?

I start with our analysis because, as former Director Dick Helms told our employees a few weeks ago, this is our "core function." As I noted earlier, it is what motivated President Truman to create a Central Intelligence Agency. Truman wanted an Agency that could pull together the relevant information from all available sources bearing upon foreign policy matters, analyze it, and provide him a timely and objective assessment, free of a policy bias.

The CIA is more vital than ever

Does the President still need such a resource at his or her disposal? Having watched the decision making process at the White House myself, the answer must be a resounding "yes." Indeed, there are far more sources of information available to a President today—and far more sources of intelligence information—than could have been imagined in 1946.

If President Truman had trouble tracking events in the age of slow moving paper, imagine coping with the fire hose of information on world events that exists today. In my view, the CIA's classic mission of separating fact from fiction and presenting analysis objectively has become only more important.

If the CIA did not pull it together, sort it out, and present it, who would? Some argue that individual agencies such as State and Defense should do it. But in my view, this would place an unfair burden on them. Our democratic system obliges these agencies to formulate policies on behalf of the President and to defend them in public and before the Congress. That is a heavy responsibility.

We also have to question whether it is realistic to assume that they also can collect and persuasively present information that would often raise questions about the very policies they espouse. That, in fact, is the role that CIA often fills as an independent source of information for the President—a source that he or she can use to evaluate the policy positions being presented.

Espionage and covert action

Earlier I asked you to consider whether support for the CIA is an investment worth making. That question can't be answered without understanding and appreciating the benefits derived from the clandestine collection of foreign intelligence. Espionage, if you will.

When many people assert we no longer need CIA, they often mean the clandestine part. Well, think about it. The goal of our clandestine collection is very simple: it is to get for the United States vital information it cannot get in any other way.

We are not out to duplicate or compete with open sources of information. Access to countries like North Korea, Iraq, Iran, and Libya is denied, and we know that these governments are trying actively to deceive us.

We may be able to discern how well they are doing in developing their capabilities or how they intend to use them by taking pictures from the air or from intercepting their communications. But I can tell you that just as frequently, a human source is the key to understanding their true intentions and capabilities.

Where does that leave us? It leaves us trying to find people on the inside—inside hostile and repressive regimes, inside drug cartels, inside terrorist groups, people who will help fill in the picture or provide the missing pieces of the puzzle. Seeking this information puts our people directly in harm's way in some of the world's most dangerous environments. So we must ask seriously, is it worth the effort and the risk entailed in trying to mount such operations? To answer that, you have to consider the magnitude of the harm that hostile states or lawless groups could potentially cause. While few may threaten our national survival, they do clearly threaten American lives.

Indeed, vital interests are often at stake in our dealings with other countries even when those countries do not threaten us with violence or military action. In those cases, we need to know if what they are telling us is true, what they say publicly as well as what they say privately. When there is reason to be skeptical of what other countries are saying to us—when we wonder what their true intentions are—we at CIA seek independent verification.

Finally, let me turn to covert action, which we define as action taken abroad to affect political, military, or economic conditions in other countries without the role of the U.S. Government being revealed or becoming apparent.

Of the CIA's major functions, covert action is by far the smallest. It is also the most controversial, both with the public and the Congress. During the 40+ years of the Cold War, Presidents frequently turned to the CIA to undertake operations to thwart the spread of Communism where diplomatic means were ineffective or unavailable, and where military action would have raised the ante to an unacceptable level.

CIA maintains a capability to carry out such operations because every President since Truman has wanted to have this option available. Moreover, Congress has wanted the President to have this option.

We can argue, of course, about how this capability has been used in the past. There have been notable failures and impressive successes. But the fact remains: our leaders have wanted this capability, and they continue to want it.

Now, as I approach the close of my remarks, I'd like to put some questions on the table with the hope that they will give concreteness to your deliberations on the "added value" that intelligence can bring to national policymaking.

Ponder if you will how important it was to the United States to know about the missiles the Soviets put into Cuba in 1962 or to understand accurately the nature of Soviet weaponry as we sought to negotiate landmark arms control agreements.

Skipping thirty years ahead, how important was it in 1992 to accurately understand North Korea's developing nuclear capability as we sought to arrest it?

And now:

How important is it, as the U.S. seeks to disrupt the flow of poisonous drugs into our country, to have arrested or captured all of the Cali druglords?

Or how valuable is it to have intelligence that helped defuse a crisis in the Taiwan strait, as was the case in 1996.

Or to accurately portray a lessening of civil strife in Rwanda just last year which made it unnecessary to place U.S. forces at risk there?

What value should we place on intelligence that has helped protect our troops in Bosnia—so that there have been no casualties to date from hostilities.

And how would world leaders have accurately documented the war crimes that occurred there without the clear intelligence provided to our policymakers and the United Nations.

How important is it to have a CIA that is able to detect those that would steal our technology secrets for economic and military gain, and to protect our critical civil infrastructure against computer terrorism.

Critics don't "get it"

The list can go on, but my point is a simple one. To those who say the CIA is just another newsgathering organization or reference service, I have to say that they just don't "get it." Our mission is not to observe, or catalog or comment, it is to warn and protect.

In a world where the U.S. has a significantly smaller military and much less global presence diplomatically than ten years ago, global intelligence reach becomes an even more critical deterrent to bad actors. The CIA gives the President and the Congress an extraordinary unilateral advantage to shape the global environment.

So how important is it to have a CIA? Vitally important.

As CIA celebrated its 50th Anniversary in September, 1998, President Bill Clinton honored us by addressing our employees. He said: "As your first customer, I depend upon your unique, accurate intelligence more than ever. Your work informs every foreign policy decision I make, from dealings with leaders in the Middle East to Russia."

"You, better than most, understand that we are not free from risks. We still need dedicated men and women to monitor foreign communications and sound the right alarms. We still need analysts to weave varied strands of data into logical, honest assessments, and, when necessary, into warnings, and we still need sophisticated counterintelligence to keep our secrets in and keep foreign agents out."

I've thought a lot about Harry Truman as I prepared this speech. In fact, I walked by his photo portrait on our ground floor the other day. The inscription he wrote below his photograph reads simply: "To the CIA—a necessity to the President of the United States—from one who knows." My fondest hope is that this conference will help the American people come to know what Harry Truman knew.

In closing, I want the American people to know that the world is safer for them because of the CIA.

I want them to know that we have a clear sense of purpose and mission.

I want them to understand that our intelligence activities are conducted in a way that is worthy of their trust, confidence, and continued support.

And I want them to know that the men and women who serve in the Intelligence Community are the very best that this nation has to offer. America should know that these men and women take serious risks every single day to protect U.S. lives and U.S. interests. They do so in silence, without public acclaim, simply for the love of their country.

17

The CIA Should Be Reformed

Melvin A. Goodman

Melvin A. Goodman is professor of international security at the National War College and senior fellow at the Center for International Policy.

The September 11, 2001, terrorist attacks on America demonstrate how ineffective the CIA has become at anticipating threats to national security. One problem with the agency is that over the years it has begun to de-emphasize information-gathering for policy-making and has become focused instead on supporting the Pentagon's war efforts. However, the CIA has proven inept at aiding the Pentagon in those tactical demands, which has resulted in a series of major intelligence disasters. To address this problem, the CIA must be separated from the Department of Defense. Another problem with the agency is that it has not fundamentally altered its methods since the end of the Cold War, yet the threats to national security have changed dramatically since the collapse of the Soviet Union. The CIA needs to develop new strategies to deal with current threats. In addition, the CIA must end its reliance on covert action. Its recruitment of unsavory characters has usually been counterproductive and has sullied the agency's reputation worldwide. The CIA must also learn to adapt to the rapid technological change characteristic of the twenty-first century.

One week after the terrorist attacks on the Pentagon and the World Trade Center, national security adviser Condoleeza Rice told the press: "This isn't Pearl Harbor." No, it's worse. Sixty years ago, the United States did not have a director of central intelligence and 13 intelligence agencies with a combined budget of more than $30 billion to produce an early warning against our enemies.

There is another significant and telling difference between Pearl Harbor and the September 11, 2001, attacks: Less than two weeks after Pearl Harbor, President Franklin D. Roosevelt appointed a high-level military and civilian commission to determine the causes of the intelligence failure. After the recent attacks, however, President George W. Bush, Direc-

From "Revamping the CIA: The Terrorist Attacks Have Once Again Exposed Wide-Ranging Flaws in the Agency's Operations," by Melvin A. Goodman, *Issues in Science Technology*, Winter 2001. Copyright © 2001 by National Academy of Sciences. Reprinted with permission.

tor of Central Intelligence George Tenet, and, surprisingly, the chairmen of the Senate and House intelligence committees adamantly opposed any investigation or post mortem. Senator Bob Graham (D-Fla.), chair of the Senate Select Committee on Intelligence, said it would not be "appropriate" to conduct an investigation at this time; his predecessor, Senator Richard Shelby (R-Ala.), agreed that any investigation could wait another year. The President's Foreign Intelligence Advisory Board normally would request such a study, but the board currently has only one member, because the president has not yet replaced members whose terms have expired. The president's failure to appoint a statutory inspector general at the Central Intelligence Agency (CIA) deprives the agency of the one individual who could have requested an investigation regardless of the CIA director's views. Overall, the unwillingness to conduct an inquiry increases the suspicion that there may have been indicators of the attacks that went unheeded.

The failure to anticipate the attacks is merely the latest in a series of CIA failures during the past 10 years. The CIA spent nearly two-thirds of its resources on the Soviet Union but did not foresee the Kremlin's collapse. Yet there was no investigation or post mortem of what went wrong in the CIA's directorate of intelligence, nor were there major changes in the CIA's analytical culture.

The failure to anticipate the [September 11, 2001, terrorist] attacks is merely the latest in a series of CIA failures.

There was also the incredible but true saga of Aldrich Ames, the CIA officer who spied for the Soviet Union and the Russian Federation for nearly a decade, flaunting his KGB-supplied wealth and betraying the entire U.S. spy network inside Moscow. The Ames saga did lead to a 1994 study of the CIA's clandestine culture that concluded, in the words of then-director James Woolsey, "It is a culture where a sense of trust and camaraderie within the fraternity can smack of elitism and arrogance." A year later, in fact, then-director John Deutch learned that the CIA payroll included a Guatemalan colonel implicated in the murder of a U.S. citizen and, as a result, initiated efforts to reform the directorate of operations and to remove the thugs from the payroll. Predictably, the old boy network rallied in the name of the directorate and tried to stymie Deutch's efforts.

Demilitarize intelligence gathering

Previous directors, particularly Deutch and Robert Gates, have done great harm to the CIA and the intelligence community by deemphasizing strategic intelligence for use in policymaking and catering instead to the tactical demands of the Pentagon. The CIA began to produce fewer national intelligence estimates and assessments that dealt with strategic matters and placed its emphasis on intelligence support for the war fighter. Gates, moreover, ended CIA analysis of key order-of-battle issues in order to avoid tendentious analytical struggles with the Pentagon; Deutch's creation of the National Imagery and Mapping Agency (NIMA) at the Department of Defense (DOD) enabled the Pentagon to be the sole interpreter of satellite photography. This is particularly important because the Pentagon uses imagery analysis to justify the defense budget, to gauge the likelihood of military conflict around the world, and to verify arms control agreements. In creating NIMA, Deutch abolished the CIA's Office of Imagery Analysis and the joint DOD-CIA National Photographic Center, which often challenged the Pentagon's analytical views.

Although the collapse of the Soviet Union . . . fundamentally altered the strategic environment, there has been no major effort to redefine U.S. national security and intelligence needs.

In its short history, NIMA has been responsible for a series of major intelligence disasters, including the failure to predict Indian nuclear testing in 1998, the bombing of the Chinese embassy in Belgrade in 1999, and more recently the exaggeration of the missile programs in North Korea and Iran. The failure to anticipate and record Indian nuclear testing stemmed from the Pentagon's downgrading of South Asian intelligence collection and DOD's low priority for counterproliferation. Open sources did a far better job of predicting the nuclear tests than did the U.S. intelligence community. To make matters worse, CIA Director Tenet told the Senate that the CIA could not monitor and verify the Comprehensive Test Ban Treaty and, for the first time in 80 years, the Senate failed to ratify a major international treaty.

The bombing of the Chinese embassy was attributed to the faulty work of NIMA as well as the inability of the CIA to conduct operational targeting for the Pentagon. Consequently, when the crew of a U.S. B-2 Stealth bomber skimmed over Yugoslavia and dropped three bombs on a building in downtown Belgrade, it actually believed that it had made a direct hit on the country's arms procurement headquarters. Instead, three people were killed and 20 wounded, creating a diplomatic crisis with Beijing and key members of the NATO coalition. The CIA had never been responsible for operational targeting before, and as a result of the Belgrade disaster, Tenet has made sure that the agency stays out of the targeting business.

Leaving imagery analysis in the Pentagon's hands allows the military to exaggerate strategic threats to the United States. Throughout the Cold War, military intelligence consistently exaggerated Soviet strategic power, particularly the quantity and quality of Soviet strategic forces and the capabilities of key weapons systems. The Air Force was particularly guilty of exaggerating Soviet missile forces, presumably in order to gain additional resources for U.S. missile deployment. At the same time, the uniformed military was not enamored with the intelligence capabilities of satellite photography and such surveillance aircraft as the U-2, and if it had not been for lobbying by the CIA and civilian scientists, the United States would not have had access to such technology until much later. When the CIA tried to create its own Foreign Missile and Space

Analysis Center in 1963 to provide detailed intelligence information on offensive missile systems, senior Air Force generals unsuccessfully tried to stop it.

New intelligence priorities

Although the collapse of the Soviet Union and its Eastern European empire fundamentally altered the strategic environment, there has been no major effort to redefine U.S. national security and intelligence needs. The Soviet collapse created new areas of instability and policy challenges in the Caucasus, central Asia, and southeastern Europe, where the United States and the intelligence community possess few intellectual resources. And nontraditional security problems, which will define U.S. policy choices in the 21st century, have been given short shrift. These problems include water scarcity in the Middle East, social migration caused by coastal flooding in South Asia, infectious diseases in Africa and Russia, and contamination caused by nuclear and chemical weapons stored in the former Soviet Union.

The CIA's favorite "freedom fighter" in Afghanistan in the 1980s . . . was also the country's chief drug lord.

The nontraditional national security problems that confront the United States could give the CIA a competitive advantage because of its data storehouse on oil reserves, demographics, and water supply. The CIA is in a position to provide information on a variety of environmental issues, using baseline data from satellite photography documenting global warming, ozone depletion, and environmental contamination. Spy satellites already provide key environmental data on Earth's diminishing grasslands, forests, and food resources. Yet the CIA has not been forthcoming with its data, and the only politician who has ever made a serious effort to obtain such data and analysis—former vice president Al Gore—is on the sidelines. To make matters worse, there is a satellite sitting on the ground that is designed to collect such data, but the Bush administration will not pay to launch it.

With the proliferation of international peacekeeping missions, the intelligence community is a natural resource for providing political and military data to peacekeepers in places such as Afghanistan, Bosnia, Cambodia, and Somalia. The CIA should have assisted the United Nations (UN) monitoring programs in Iraq rather than running its own operations against Saddam Hussein. War crimes tribunals also require funds and expertise for collecting data on political and military officials, which would be a less difficult task if the political and biographic assets of the CIA could be used. And it is unlikely that global institutions such as the International Atomic Energy Agency can successfully monitor strategic weapons production in North Korea, Iraq, and Pakistan without support from the CIA.

Unfortunately, the CIA has shown little inclination to take on these tasks. Woolsey was lukewarm at best to the idea of sharing intelligence with international agencies. Deutch was stubbornly opposed to providing information to the UN, even though it would have been helpful in peacekeeping situations. And current director Tenet also does not have much interest in these activities.

Problems with covert action

There is no absolute political and ethical guideline delineating when to engage in covert action. However, Cyrus Vance, secretary of state in the Carter administration, articulated a standard two decades ago when he recommended covert action only when "absolutely essential" to the national security of the United States and when "no other means" would do. The CIA observed this standard in the breach when it placed world-class criminals such as Panama's General Manuel Noriega, Guatemala's Colonel Julio Alpirez, Peru's intelligence chief Vladimiro Montesinos, and Chile's General Manuel Contreras on its payroll. The CIA's favorite "freedom fighter" in Afghanistan in the 1980s, Gulbuddin Hekmatyar, was also the country's chief drug lord.

In addition to playing a role in overthrowing the democratically elected government of Chile in the 1970s, the CIA hired and protected Contreras despite his involvement in assassination plots in South America and the United States, including the car bombing in the nation's capital of former Chilean Ambassador Orlando Letelier and his U.S. associate, Ronni Karpen Moffitt. Recently released documents demonstrate that the CIA placed Contreras on its payroll despite its acknowledgement that he was the "principal obstacle to a reasonable human rights policy" in Chile.

These unsavory assets had nothing to do with the collection of sensitive intelligence but were important to the CIA for the conduct of covert actions in South America that usually were counterproductive to the interests of the countries involved as well as to the United States. Montesinos, for example, was responsible for two decades of human rights abuses in Peru. Yet the CIA helped him flee the country in September 2000 to avoid standing trial for crimes that included the massacre of innocent civilians in the early 1990s. The CIA station in Amman approved an arms deal between Jordanian officials and Montesinos, although he was involved in a 1998 transfer of arms from Jordan to leftist guerrillas in Colombia, perhaps Washington's most notorious enemies in Latin America. There is probably no stronger evidence of the ineptitude of the CIA's directorate of operations.

The CIA will no longer be on the cutting edge of advanced technology.

We learned in 1999 that the United States and the CIA used the cover of the UN and the UN Special Commission (UNSCOM) to conduct a secret operation to spy on Iraqi military communications as part of an effort to topple Saddam Hussein. Neither the UN nor UNSCOM had authorized the U.S. surveillance, which Hussein cited as justification for expelling the UN operation. As a result, the most successful effort to monitor and verify Iraq's nuclear, chemical, and biological programs was lost, and the credibility of multilateral inspection teams around the world was compromised.

Separating intelligence and operations

Any reform of the role and missions of the CIA must recognize that the agency performs two very different functions. The CIA's clandestine operations, particularly covert action, are part of the policy process. Yet when paid agency assets are also the sources of intelligence reporting, the finished reports may be seriously flawed. CIA's covert operations are approved and often designed by the White House and the State Department to support specific policies. The Bay of Pigs in 1961, which the inspector general of the CIA described as the "perfect failure," and Iran-Contra in the 1980s, which violated U.S. law, demonstrated the ability of the directorate of operations to corrupt the analysis of the directorate of intelligence.

The CIA's intelligence analysis, including national estimates and current reporting, must provide both an objective exploration of the situation for which policy is required and an impartial assessment of alternative policy options. Intelligence should play a role in setting the context for policy formulation, but it should never become an advocate for a specific policy. CIA Director William Casey and his deputy for intelligence, Robert Gates, slanted intelligence reporting in the 1980s to support operational activity in Central America and southwest Asia. In his memoirs, former Secretary of State George Shultz charged that the CIA's operational involvement "colored" the agency's estimates and analysis. The CIA's distortion of Soviet strategic policy skewed the public debate on the Star Wars program[1] in the 1980s, and similar distortions of the strategic capabilities of so-called rogue states have factored into the debate on national missile defense.

The decline of wizardry

During the worst days of the Cold War, the strategic position of the United States was enhanced by the scientific and technological successes of the CIA, which designed and operated some of our most important spy satellites as well as the U-2 spy plane. The CIA was heavily involved in the collection of signals intelligence and helped pioneer the technical analysis of foreign missile and space programs. Secret CIA installations eavesdropped on Soviet missile tests and gathered intelligence that was crucial to the success of arms control negotiations in the 1970s and 1980s. As a result, the CIA had advance knowledge of every Soviet strategic weapons system and up-to-date intelligence on the capabilities of these systems.

Unfortunately, the technological frontier has moved from [CIA headquarters in] Langley, Virginia, to Silicon Valley, and as a result, the CIA has lost much of its technological edge. In 1998, the CIA abolished its Office of Research and Development (ORD), which had been responsible for much of the agency's success in the fields of technical collection and an-

1. President Ronald Reagan intended to develop a new system to reduce the threat of a nuclear attack by the Soviet Union. The original mission was scrapped in 1987.

alytical intelligence. The CIA will no longer be on the cutting edge of advanced technology in the fields of clandestine collection and satellite reconnaissance and will be heavily dependent on the technology of outside contractors. ORD led the way in major breakthroughs in the area of overhead reconnaissance, including optics and imagery interpretation, which presumably are paying dividends in Afghanistan. Previous ORD technology, such as sophisticated facial recognition, will help in the war against terrorism but only if that technology is shared with the Immigration and Naturalization Service (INS), the FBI, and the Drug Enforcement Agency.

The decline of the CIA during the past decade coincides with reduced oversight of the intelligence community.

In addition to the weakening of the CIA in important areas of science and technology, the National Security Agency (NSA), which is responsible for collecting and interpreting signals and communications intelligence from around the world, has been weakened by a series of management decisions that have created serious problems. The NSA has been caught off guard by a series of new communications technologies that have compromised its intercept capabilities, including fiber optic cables that cannot be tapped, encryption software that cannot be broken, and cell phone traffic that is too voluminous to be processed. There is no question that a managerial revolution needs to take place throughout the intelligence community.

A new intelligence infrastructure

What the CIA and the intelligence community should be, what they should do, and what they should prepare to do are all less clear than at any time since the end of World War II and the beginning of the Cold War. Throughout the Cold War, the need to count and characterize Soviet weapons systems against which U.S. forces might find themselves engaged, as well as the search for indications of surprise attack, focused the CIA's efforts. Such clarity disappeared with the fall of the Soviet Union. The following steps are needed in order to design an intelligence infrastructure to deal effectively with the new and emerging national security problems.

Demilitarize the intelligence community. The mismatch between the tools of the past and the missions of the future has given rise to an increased militarization of the various intelligence agencies and an excessive reliance on CIA support for the war fighter. It is essential that the major intelligence collection agencies—NIMA, NSA, and the National Reconnaissance Office (which designs spy satellites), with their collective budget of at least $10 billion—be taken from DOD and transferred to a new office that reports to the director of central intelligence. This move would allow more leeway for spending the intelligence budget on analysis and sharing of information gathered by satellites, rather than the current emphasis on building satellites and other data collectors. According to press reports, retired general Brent Scowcroft, who is conducting a comprehensive review of the intelligence community for President Bush, favors such a transfer of authority, but Secretary of Defense Donald Rumsfeld and high-ranking members of the Senate Armed Forces Committee oppose it.

Revive oversight. The decline of the CIA during the past decade coincides with reduced oversight of the intelligence community by the Senate and House intelligence committees. Beginning with the chairmanship of Senator Shelby in 1994, the Senate committee has become less effective in providing oversight and in advancing much-needed reform. It is unusual to have more than two or three senators present at any given time, even at important hearings, and Senate committee members are limited to an eight-year term. (The House has a six-year term limit.) The number of open intelligence oversight hearings has dropped significantly, as has the number of non-governmental witnesses invited to testify. Because the authorization bill for the intelligence community is imbedded in the defense budget, the Senate Armed Forces Committee is able to significantly modify the authorizations of the intelligence committee. The system worked when former Senators Sam Nunn and David Boren, who were close colleagues, chaired the armed services and intelligence committees, respectively, in the 1980s, but the system has broken down in the 1990s. The House intelligence committee chair, Representative Porter Goss (R-Fla.), is a former CIA case officer who has acted as an advocate for the intelligence community and not a reformer.

CIA propaganda has had little effect on foreign audiences and should end immediately.

There has also been an astonishing exchange of personnel between intelligence committee staffs and the agencies they oversee. Tenet and his chief of staff formerly served as the majority and minority staff chiefs, respectively, of the Senate intelligence committee. Other staff members went on to serve in a variety of other CIA posts: inspector general, chief of the legislative counsel's office, chief of the Foreign Broadcast Information Service, deputy director of the Counter-Proliferation Center, and director of resource management for the directorate of operations. The current head of the NRO and the NRO's inspector general both came from the Senate intelligence committee, as did the deputy director of intelligence programs at the National Security Council. It is unprecedented for one congressional committee to supply staff to so many senior positions at a major executive agency, which raises a disturbing question:

Who will oversee the overseers?

Reduce covert action. Covert action could be radically reduced without compromising national security. CIA propaganda has had little effect on foreign audiences and should end immediately. The CIA should never be allowed to interfere in foreign elections.

Many problems that have been considered candidates for covert action were ultimately addressed openly by unilateral means or cooperatively through international measures, both of which are preferable to clandestine operations. Nuclear proliferation problems created by missile programs in Iraq and North Korea in the 1990s led to congressional calls for covert actions, but in both cases overt multilateral activity with the United States in a pivotal role contributed to denuclearization. The U.S. military was successfully involved in secret denuclearization of the former Soviet Union, clandestinely removing strategic weapons and nuclear materials from Georgia, Kazakhstan, and Moldova in the 1990s.

The CIA must strengthen links across the intelligence community in order to share intelligence.

Separate operations and analysis. It is time to debate whether it is preferable to separate the CIA's operational activity from its analytical work or continue running the risk of tainted intelligence. The issue is one of advocacy, ensuring that the provider of intelligence is not in a position to advance its own point of view in the policy process. The CIA's heavy policy involvement in the war on terrorism will certainly call into question the worst-case views of the directorate of intelligence on terrorist threats at home and abroad.

Because there are few institutional safeguards for impartial and objective analysis, the intelligence community ultimately depends on professional personnel of the highest intellectual and moral caliber. Yet editor and essayist Walter Lippmann reminded us more than 70 years ago that [it] is essential to "separate as absolutely as it is possible to do so the staff which executes from the staff which investigates." If Washington is serious about "reinventing government," Lippmann's admonition is a good place to start for the intelligence community.

The intelligence directorate has become far too large and unwieldy and, because of its failures during the past decade, has become permeated with the fear of being wrong or second-guessed. Hiring smarter, more informed people would help. In recent years, the CIA's rigorous security standards have often filtered out analysts who have traveled and lived abroad and have collegial relations with their foreign counterparts. Not surprisingly, the intelligence directorate thus lacks people with the language skills and the regional expertise needed for dealing with today's intelligence challenges.

The operations directorate also needs to be revamped. Its modus operandi is based on placing relatively junior people abroad, working out of U.S. embassies with State Department cover. Yet the directorate will not be able to substantially increase the amount of crucial information it collects unless it is willing to take greater risks by assigning experienced people abroad without diplomatic cover. Only then would intelligence personnel have the wherewithal to encounter the unsavory people who threaten our interests. In addition, the operations directorate must rely more heavily on foreign liaison services that have access to sensitive intelligence on terrorism and criminal activities abroad. Doing so would allow the CIA to concentrate clandestine collection efforts on countries where no access currently exists, such as Somalia, Sudan, and Yemen.

Just as the U.S. military could be used to perform clandestine actions in wartime, State Department foreign service officers could collect intelligence more effectively than their clandestine counterparts. However, recent budget cuts have seriously eroded the department's capabilities. At the same time, the demands of an unstable and fractious world have created additional demands on the department, which must supply an ambassador and staff to 192 independent countries. Because of budget cutbacks, the department has been forced to close important posts in Zagreb, Medellin, Lahore, Alexandria, and Johannesburg, to name just a few, and has had to post political amateurs with deep pockets to key embassies in Europe and Asia. The staffs of most of these embassies could collect intelligence openly and less expensively than could their CIA counterparts, freeing the agency to concentrate on the collection of intelligence on terrorist networks, technology, and weapons of mass destruction in closed areas. One of the CIA's first and most prestigious directors, Allen Dulles, emphasized that "the bulk of intelligence can be obtained through overt channels" and that if the agency grew to be a "great big octopus" it would not function well. The CIA has about 16,000 employees—more than four times as many as the State Department.

Increase intelligence sharing. The CIA must strengthen links across the intelligence community in order to share intelligence. Today, information tends to move vertically within each of the 13 intelligence agencies instead of horizontally across them. The CIA's emphasis on the compartmentalization of intelligence and the need to know also serve as obstacles to intelligence sharing. In addition, the CIA must become more generous in sharing information with organizations that will be on the front lines in the war against terrorism, including the INS, the Federal Aviation Agency, the Border Guards, and the Coast Guard.

The intelligence community, particularly the CIA, faces a situation comparable only to that of 55 years ago, when President Truman created the CIA and the National Security Council. As in 1947 and 1948, the international environment has been fundamentally recast and the threats have been fundamentally altered. The institutions created to fight the Cold War must be redesigned. This is exactly the task that the new FBI director, Robert Mueller, has established for himself and his agency, and a failure to do so at the CIA could mean a repeat of the intelligence failures of September 11, 2001, and an additional erosion of CIA credibility. A reconstituted directorate of operations and directorate of intelligence could be the linchpin of a reform process that will restore a central and valued role to intelligence in the making of national security policy.

Organizations to Contact

The editors have compiled the following list of organizations concerned with the issues debated in this book. The descriptions are derived from materials provided by the organizations. All have publications or information available for interested readers. The list was compiled on the date of publication of the present volume; names, addresses, phone and fax numbers, and e-mail and Internet addresses may change. Be aware that many organizations take several weeks or longer to respond to inquiries, so allow as much time as possible.

American Civil Liberties Union (ACLU)
125 Broad St., 18th Floor, New York, NY 10004-2400
(212) 549-2500
e-mail: aclu@aclu.org • website: www.aclu.org

The American Civil Liberties Union is a national organization that works to defend Americans' civil rights guaranteed by the U.S. Constitution, arguing that measures to protect national security should not compromise fundamental civil liberties. It publishes and distributes policy statements, pamphlets, and press releases with titles such as "In Defense of Freedom in a Time of Crisis."

American Enterprise Institute (AEI)
1150 17th St. NW, Washington, DC 20036
(202) 862-5800 • fax: (202) 862-7177
website: www.aei.org

The American Enterprise Institute for Public Policy Research is a scholarly research institute that is dedicated to preserving limited government, private enterprise, and a strong foreign policy and national defense. It publishes books, including *Study of Revenge: The First World Trade Center Attack* and *Saddam Hussein's War Against America.* Articles about terrorism and the September 11, 2001, terrorist attacks can be found in its magazine, *American Enterprise,* and on its website.

The Brookings Institution
1775 Massachusetts Ave. NW, Washington, DC 20036
(202) 797-6000 • fax: (202) 797-6004
e-mail: brookinfo@brook.edu • website: www.brookings.org

The Brookings Institution, founded in 1927, is a think tank that conducts research and education in foreign policy, economics, government, and the social sciences. In 2001 it began America's Response to Terrorism, a project that provides briefings and analysis to the public and which is featured on the center's website. Other publications include the quarterly *Brookings Review*, periodic *Policy Briefs*, and books, including *Terrorism and U.S. Foreign Policy.*

Center for Defense Information
1779 Massachusetts Ave. NW, Suite 615, Washington, DC 20036
(202) 332-0600 • fax: (202) 462-4559
e-mail: info@cdi.org • website: www.cdi.org

The Center for Defense Information is a nonpartisan, nonprofit organization that researches all aspects of global security. It seeks to educate the public and policymakers about issues such as weapons systems, security policy, and defense budgeting. It publishes the monthly publication *Defense Monitor* and the study "Homeland Security: A Competitive Strategies Approach."

Central Intelligence Agency (CIA)
Office of Public Affairs
Washington, DC 20505
(703) 482-0623 • fax: (703) 482-1739
website: www.cia.gov

The CIA was created in 1947 with the signing of the National Security Act (NSA) by President Harry S. Truman. The NSA charged the Director of Central Intelligence (DCI) with coordinating the nation's intelligence activities and correlating, evaluating, and disseminating intelligence that affects national security. The CIA is an independent agency, responsible to the president through the DCI, and accountable to the American people through the Intelligence Oversight Committee of the U.S. Congress. Publications, including *Factbook on Intelligence and Report of Investigation—Volume II: The Contra Story,* are available on its website.

Federal Bureau of Investigation (FBI)
935 Pennsylvania Ave. NW, Room 7972, Washington, DC 20535
(202) 324-3000
website: www.fbi.gov

The FBI, the principal investigative arm of the U.S. Department of Justice, evolved from an unnamed force of Special Agents formed on July 26, 1908. It has the authority and responsibility to investigate specific crimes assigned to it. The FBI also is authorized to provide other law enforcement agencies with cooperative services, such as fingerprint identification, laboratory examinations, and police training. The mission of the FBI is to uphold the law through the investigation of violations of federal criminal law; to protect the United States from foreign intelligence and terrorist activities; to provide leadership and law enforcement assistance to federal, state, local, and international agencies; and to perform these responsibilities in a manner that is responsive to the needs of the public and is faithful to the Constitution of the United States. Press releases, congressional statements, and major speeches on issues concerning the FBI are available on the agency's website.

Human Rights Watch
350 Fifth Ave., 34th Floor, New York, NY 10118-3299
(212) 290-4700 • fax: (212) 736-1300
e-mail: hrwnyc@hrw.org • website: www.hrw.org

Human Rights Watch monitors and reports human rights abuses in the United States and internationally. It sponsors fact-finding missions, disseminates results, and publishes the bimonthly *Human Rights Watch* newsletter. Information about the U.S. government's response to the September 11, 2001, terrorist attacks and its impact on human rights is available on its website.

Institute for Policy Studies (IPS)
733 15th St. NW, Suite 1020, Washington, DC 20005
(202) 234-9382 • fax: (202) 387-7915
website: www.ips-dc.org

The Institute for Policy Studies is a progressive think tank that works to develop societies built around the values of justice and nonviolence. It publishes reports, including *Global Perspectives: A Media Guide to Foreign Policy Experts.* Numerous articles and interviews on the September 11, 2001, terrorist attacks and on terrorism generally are available on its website.

National Security Agency
9800 Savage Road, Ft. Meade, MD 20755-6248
(301) 688-6524
website: www.nsa.gov

The National Security Agency coordinates, directs, and performs activities such as designing cipher systems, which protect American information systems, and produce foreign intelligence information. It is the largest employer of mathematicians in the United States and also hires the nation's best codemakers and codebreakers. Speeches, briefings, and reports are available on its website.

Bibliography

Books

Robert Baer	*See No Evil: The True Story of a Ground Soldier in the CIA's War on Terrorism.* New York: Crown Publishers, 2002.
Alexander Cockburn	*White Out: The CIA, Drugs, and the Press.* New York: Verso Press, 1998.
James X. Dempsey	*Terrorism and the Constitution: Sacrificing Civil Liberties in the Name of National Security.* Washington, DC: First Amendment Foundation, 2002.
Pete Earley	*Confessions of a Spy: The Real Story of Aldrich Ames.* New York: G.P. Putnam, 1997.
Craig Eisendrath, ed.	*National Insecurity: U.S. Intelligence After the Cold War.* Philadelphia: Temple University Press, 2000.
James F. Hoge and Gideon Rose, eds.	*How Did This Happen?: Terrorism and the New War.* New York: PublicAffairs, 2001.
Arthur S. Hulnick and Richard R. Valcourt	*Fixing the Spy Machine: Preparing American Intelligence for the Twenty-First Century.* Westport, CT: Praeger, 1999.
Mark Lowenthal	*Intelligence: From Secrets to Policy.* Washington, DC: Congressional Quarterly Books, 1999.
Angus MacKenzie	*Secrets: The CIA's War at Home.* Berkeley: University of California Press, 1997.
Antonio J. Mendez	*The Master of Disguise: My Secret Life in the CIA.* Grand Haven, MI: Brilliance Corporation, 1999.
Paul R. Pillar	*Terrorism and U.S. Foreign Policy.* Washington, DC: Brookings Institute, 2002.
Jeffrey T. Richelson	*The Wizards of Langley: Inside the CIA's Directorate of Science and Technology.* Boulder, CO: Westview Press, 2002.
Frances Stoner Saunders	*The Cultural Cold War: The CIA and the World of Arts and Letters.* New York: New Press, 2000.
Robert David Steele	*On Intelligence: Spies and Secrecy in an Open World.* Fairfax, VA: AFCEA International Press, 2000.
Joseph J. Trento	*The Secret History of the CIA.* Roseville, CA: Prima Publishing, 2001.
Gary Webb	*Dark Alliance: The CIA, the Contras, and the Crack Cocaine Explosion.* New York: Seven Stories Press, 1998.
Amy B. Zegart	*Flawed by Design: The Evolution of the CIA, JCS, and NSC.* Stanford, CA: Stanford University Press, 1999.

Periodicals

Helle Bering — "Earth to CIA," *Washington Times*, October 3, 2001.

Bruce Berkowitz and Allan E. Goodman — "The Logic of Covert Action," *National Interest*, Spring 1998.

Charles Bowden — "The Pariah," *Esquire*, September 1998.

John M. Deutch and Jeffrey H. Smith — "Smarter Intelligence," *Foreign Policy*, January/February 2002.

Robert Dreyfuss — "Dim Intelligence," *American Prospect*, October 22, 2001.

Bob Drogin — "CIA Quandry: Just How Far Can Its Tactics Go?" *Seattle Times*, October 28, 2001.

Reuel Marc Gerecht — "The Counterterrorist Myth," *Atlantic Monthly*, July/August 2001.

Bill Gertz — "CIA Rethinks Rules That Limit Recruits," *Washington Times*, January 24, 2002.

Melvin A. Goodman — "Covert Operations Unnecessary in a Post–Cold War World," *San Diego Union-Tribune*, May 4, 1997.

Brian Hansen — "Intelligence Reforms," *CQ Researcher*, January 25, 2002.

John Hillen — "Know Knothings: U.S. Intelligence Failures Stem from Too Much Information, Not Enough Understanding," *National Review*, August 3, 1998.

Joel Himelfarb — "The Agency That Failed: The CIA's Non-War on Terror," *Washington Times*, April 16, 2002.

Frederick P. Hitz — "Unleashing the Rogue Elephant: September 11 and Letting the CIA Be the CIA," *Harvard Journal of Law and Public Policy*, Spring 2002.

Issues and Controversies On File — "Ethics of Intelligence Gathering," November 23, 2001.

Rhodri Jeffrey-Jones — "The CIA Con-Trick," *History Today*, December 2001.

Timothy W. Maier and Sean Paige — "Does America Need the CIA?" *Insight on the News*, August 17, 1998.

Abraham McLaughlin — "CIA Expands Its Watchful Eye to the U.S.," *Christian Science Monitor*, December 17, 2001.

Abraham H. Miller — "The CIA and Crack Cocaine Story: Fact or Fiction?" *World & I*, February 1998.

Robert Scheer — "CIA's Tracks Lead in Disastrous Circle," *Los Angeles Times*, September 17, 2001.

Lawrence B. Sulc — "Can the CIA Be Fixed?" *World & I*, September 1998.

Jacob Sullum — "License to Kill," *Reason*, September 22, 2001.

Evan Thomas and John Barry — "Evil in the Cross Hairs," *Newsweek*, December 24, 2001.

J. Michael Waller — "Blinded Vigilance," *Insight on the News*, October 15, 2001.

Tim Weiner — "CIA's Expanded Powers Place Spies on U.S. Soil," *Seattle Times*, January 20, 2002.

Index